Richard Beeston began his long and distinguished career as a foreign correspondent working for a clandestine Arabic radio station run by MI6 during the Suez War. From 1961 to 1986 he was the *Daily Telegraph*'s correspondent for Beirut, Nairobi, Moscow and Washington and in the late 1980s the *Daily Mail*'s Washington correspondent. He has covered many significant world events, including the collapse of the Belgian Congo, East Africa's post-independence upheavals, Middle East revolutions, the Vietnam War, Watergate and the Soviet invasion of Afghanistan. Since 1990 he has worked as a freelance writer for *The Times*, the *Daily Telegraph* and *Saga Magazine*. He also writes obituaries for *The Times* covering statesmen, politicians, diplomats and crooks – specializing in the Middle East, Russia and the USA.

Moyra, Jennifer, Fiona and Richard –
my good companions

To Rose
With best
Wishes

[signature]
5 Feb 07

Tauris Parke Paperbacks is an imprint of I.B.Tauris. It is dedicated to publishing books in accessible paperback editions for the serious general reader within a wide range of categories, including biography, history, travel and the ancient world. The list includes select, critically acclaimed works of top quality writing by distinguished authors that continue to challenge, to inform and to inspire. These are books that possess those subtle but intrinsic elements that mark them out as something exceptional.

The Colophon of Tauris Parke Paperbacks is a representation of the ancient Egyptian ibis, sacred to the god Thoth, who was himself often depicted in the form of this most elegant of birds. Thoth was credited in antiquity as the scribe of the ancient Egyptian gods and as the inventor of writing and was associated with many aspects of wisdom and learning.

LOOKING FOR TROUBLE

The Life and Times of a Foreign Correspondent

RICHARD BEESTON

TPP

TAURIS PARKE
PAPERBACKS

Published in 2006 by Tauris Parke Paperbacks
An imprint of I.B.Tauris and Co Ltd
6 Salem Road, London W2 4BU
175 Fifth Avenue, New York NY 10010
www.ibtauris.com

In the United States of America and Canada distributed by Palgrave Macmillan a
division of St. Martin's Press
175 Fifth Avenue, New York NY 10010

First published in 1997 by Brassey's

Cover image: Richard Beeston, Cyprus

ISBN 10: 1 84511 277 6
ISBN 13: 978 1 84511 277 6

A full CIP record for this book is available from the British Library
A full CIP record is available from the Library of Congress

Library of Congress Catalog Card Number: available

Printed and bound in India by Replika Press Pvt. Ltd.

Contents

List of Plates

Foreword to the
Second Edition

'There can be no better avocation for a newspaperman,' said the Editor, crossing his arms and looking across his desk at me in a quizzical fashion, 'than that of foreign correspondent.'

The writer is William Le Queux, Edwardian pulp fiction writer and, of course, journalist; the passage comes from one of his autobiographical books. Everyone who has ever worked for a newspaper knows the Editor was absolutely right. In the past, at any rate, the foreign correspondent was as grand as an ambassador, and had access to all sorts of secrets and privileged information. It was an impossibly glamorous job, and the people who did it were themselves impossibly glamorous.

Richard Beeston was the archetype of the foreign correspondent: clever, well-informed, and somehow born to the role. And what a career he had! His was the by-line from dozens of difficult places; and for a foreign correspondent, the greater the difficulty of the place, the more interesting it was. His career began at the height of the great age of the newspaper correspondent. He followed it through all its changes to the beginning of its decline with the end of the cold war. That was when foreign reporting, began to decline: just as the spy novel, and our sense of relative national security, also declined. Richard Beeston, having been an ornament of the Golden Age of newspaper correspondence, was lucky not to have experienced its Age of Brass.

Once upon a time the *Daily Express* and the *Daily Mail* vied for the best reporting of wars and crises abroad; even the *Daily Mirror* had a good foreign desk and good correspondents. It is almost impossible to imagine such a thing nowadays. Richard's main area of operation was the big diplomatic story, but like all good newspapermen he could turn his hand to a disaster, or even to a society event of some kind. He was the kind of journalist of whom his sub-editing colleagues back in Fleet Street, which still existed as the home of the British newspaper, would say enviously, 'He writes like an angel.'

Richard did indeed: you can see it in this delightful book. But he had all the other qualities of the first-class foreign correspondent too, including the ability to get on with the people who mattered, and keep them as friends and contacts forever more.

When I first met Richard, in his beautifully furnished flat in Moscow in, I suppose, 1978, he told me the story of how he came to be living there. It is much too good for me to spoil here, but it concerns his friendship with Kim Philby, a freezing Russian winter, and the Bolshoi. I confess to having dined out on it for nearly thirty years, as I was told it that summer's day in Moscow, with a glass of the Beestons' famous gin and tonic in my hand.

Richard and Moyra, like a few of the other great journalistic couples, have created a dynasty. They had the great pleasure of seeing the by-line still appearing in the British national press through Richard, their son, who is the diplomatic editor of *The Times*.

This is a delightful book, which opens up a world that is already starting to recede into the past, even though it is still so close to us in time: the era of the portable 'Imperial', of the telex, of the microphone in the ceiling and the spy at the door. To those who cannot remember such a time it is an eye-opener. To those of us who can, it is a pure joy.

John Simpson,
Paris, October 2005

Preface

The late 1950s, when I began a career as a foreign correspondent, was an age before computers, mobile phones and instant satellite communications. We went to wars and revolutions in our drip-dry suits and button-down shirts – armed with a note book and an Olivetti portable typewriter. For us there were no steel helmets, flack jackets and armoured plated cars and the concept of a colleague being 'embedded' would have been interpreted in quite a different way.

In those more innocent days we somehow managed an amateur and neutral status, and were unlikely to become the target of hostage-takers or the victims of religious fanatics. The twenty-first century is a more dangerous time, reflected in the high rate of casualties suffered by reporters and photographers in upheavals in the post-communist world.

Communications were the biggest headache in covering events in the third world – largely the Middle East and Africa – usually related to post-colonial unrest fuelled by cold war rivalries. Getting the story was often the easiest part. Then you typed it out as a telegram, counted the words, searched out the censor and a god-forsaken post office and cabled it off with a prayer and a bribe to the operator.

Alternatively you could spend all day waiting for a phone line to London and, if you did get through risk being abruptly cut off. As a last resort you could hang around the airport hoping to find some kindly traveller who would pocket your dispatch and 'pigeon' it out of the country.

A big advantage for the print journalist in those days was the absence of competition from television. The exclusive you had just filed would last until tomorrow morning's paper, whereas for a TV team it took days to ship and process film. Now with instant communications, tomorrow morning's story is likely to turn up on tonight's TV news-cast.

The hard core of newspaper foreign correspondents were quite a small group – usually less than a dozen on a big story – and were not just limited to the serious broadsheets. We all knew each other well, worked and drank together and cooperated, within the limits of newspaper rivalry. Some even became celebrities as television reporters, as John Simpson and Martin Bell are today.

Most of us agreed that the foreign correspondent's job beats working – or having to grow up.

London, 2006

Foreword to the
First Edition

Towards the end of 1979, Dick Beeston and I had lunch together in London. He was taking a short break from Moscow, where he was *The Daily Telegraph* correspondent. I was that newspaper's editor. 'I've been invited to visit Finland soon', I told him. 'Why not come on from there to Moscow?' he suggested.

There was, he explained, a train which pulled out of Helsinki at about three o'clock in the afternoon, crossed the Russian border at dusk, and landed up in Moscow at about breakfast the following morning. I decided to go.

It was a romantic journey through the Russian night, via Leningrad. They brought to my apartment bread, liver sausage and quarter of a bottle of vodka to add comfort to my journey. We rolled into Moscow on the dot of 9am.

Would Dick Beeston be there to meet me? During the last hours of my train journey, I occasionally fell to wondering what I would do if we missed each other at the station.

All was well. He was there. Our only handicap was that in the dirtiest of weathers, the windscreen wipers on his car were not functioning. But we made it. It was a great trip. We spent part of a day with *Pravda*, an evening with the Bolshoi. More liver sausage – but with champagne rather than vodka.

Early one morning in his flat, Dick Beeston brought me a cup of tea and a wireless which carried BBC Overseas. In Britain, I heard, rubbish was piling up in the streets during what was described as 'the winter of discontent', I listened to all this and then felt moved to observe at breakfast to Dick and his wife: 'I think we may have an election soon'.

So we did, and Mrs Thatcher entered the scene. Thus, I have always associated the Beeston household in Moscow with what was indisputably a sea-change in this country. I link him to a memorable journey – and a big slice of our modern history.

All that apart, Dick Beeston gave one quarter of a century of service to *The Daily Telegraph* in one capacity or another. In my opinion, the reporter heads the pack in any newspaper office; and the foreign correspondent, so often called upon suddenly to cover the impossible story, comes just ahead of him.

Lord Deedes, Kent, May 1997

1

Cyprus

The Approach

It was just after the Suez fiasco and I was back in London from Beirut looking for a job when Frank, a friend from MI6, contacted me.

I had spent the past four years working as a correspondent for an undercover Arabic broadcasting station based in Cyprus. Unknown to most of its staff, it came under the authority of the Secret Intelligence Service (SIS), and brought me indirectly in touch with the shadowy world of British intelligence in the Middle East. In late 1956, however, as a result of Suez, the radio station had suddenly, and rather dramatically, folded. Frank, who was fairly senior, had been posted back from Lebanon to his headquarters in London, and I was about to start looking round Fleet Street for a newspaper job.

Frank was a tall, lanky ex-schoolmaster who chain-smoked through a long cigarette holder. We met at his club, the Naval and Military, but over lunch he gave me no idea why he had asked me to come. Later, however, as we settled in a quiet corner, in deep leather arm chairs, over coffee and brandy, he became more confidential and told me he had a special reason for asking me to lunch.

Suddenly it all seemed to become clear. I was about to be recruited! An agent of the SIS in the Arab world. After all, I had been the Middle East correspondent for a clandestine radio, and knew the area and the intelligence network. I was out of a job. I was an obvious choice.

But it would be a difficult decision. From the age of 15, when I had been a penny-a-liner on a provincial paper, I had chosen journalism as my career. I had no particular wish to be a spy. From what I had seen of the profession, it was a good deal less romantic and a lot more bureaucratic than Ian Fleming made it appear. On the other hand, I

1

had a wife and two children and a flat in Beirut and no job in sight. And British agents abroad seemed to live rather well.

These considerations flashed through my mind as Frank finally came to the point. 'Look Dick', he said. 'After the Suez balls-up, I'm getting fed up with this life. What do you think of my chances of getting a job in journalism?'

Escape

Frank, depressed and demoralised by the Suez invasion, nevertheless stayed on with the firm. My own job problem was solved shortly afterwards when I was taken on by that nice old Liberal paper, the *News Chronicle* as their Middle East correspondent.

I knew from the start that quite the best job in journalism was to become a foreign corespondent. A pleasant way of life thousands of miles away from your editor, being paid to rove around the world at someone else's expense. It sounds almost too good to be true, but that's just how it was.

For a year or so, I was diverted from this goal by a job with a public relations firm in Mayfair. But towards the end of 1951, when I was 25, I saw an escape – a notice in a newspaper trade magazine advertising for an assistant editor for an Arabic broadcasting station based in Cyprus.

London was a drab and grey place in those days. There was still rationing, and apart from the absence of bombs and barrage balloons, the war might still have been on. An island in the Mediterranean seemed the answer.

Soon my wife Moyra and I were dining at the Junior Carlton with Tommy, a dapper, affable ex-military man, apparently from the Foreign Office. Tommy seemed unconcerned about my total lack of knowledge of the Arab world or even of broadcasting. He appeared far more interested however, in whether we used the right knives and forks and how much drink we could take without falling into the pudding. Alcohol, it emerged, was a problem for a number of that little band of British exiles who staffed the Near East Arab Broadcasting Station (NEABS) in Cyprus.

Perhaps a strongish head for drink compensated for my lack of qualifications. Anyhow, we passed Tommy's vetting, but were given only the vaguest of ideas about the identity of our employer or who was to pay our modest salary. However, it was the breakthrough I had been looking for – my first step on the road to over 30 carefree years as a foreign correspondent which included my *Chronicle* days in

Beirut and my time as bureau chief for *The Daily Telegraph* in Nairobi, Moscow and Washington.

Arrival in Cyprus

Britain took over Cyprus from the Ottoman Empire in 1878, inheriting an island in the Eastern Mediterranean which was deeply divided between Greeks and a 20 per cent Turkish minority, many descended from Ottoman slaves. The main political movement, dominated by the Greek Orthodox Church and a constant source of tension, was *ENOSIS* (union with Greece). It was largely non-violent until 1955 when a Greek general, George Grivas arrived with a supply of arms and launched a campaign of terrorism which eventually led to independence in August 1960.

Cyprus, when I arrived there, was a pleasant, sleepy backwater of Britain's shrinking empire, sunk in colonial lethargy. Britain was the dominant power of the region with 80,000 troops in Suez, obedient monarchies in Iraq and Jordan and control of most of the Middle East oil.

Over the next few years, as I was to witness, all this was to change, and at an alarming pace. Cyprus was soon plunged into a brutal guerrilla war of independence, Britain was swept out of Egypt and humiliated in the Suez war, the Iraqi monarchy was overthrown and decades of British domination in the Arab world collapsed. But as I landed at Nicosia airport in the autumn of 1951, I was the last person to be aware of the awesome events about to descend. After all, Winston Churchill had just returned to power, and he had Anthony Eden to look after his foreign affairs.

The flight to Cyprus in those days was a leisurely, civilised affair. Take off at about 10am from London, arrive in Rome in the late afternoon, spend a night at the Quirinale Hotel as a guest of BOAC, breakfast in Rome and land in Nicosia that evening. I was met by a rather boozy member of the radio station – the finance officer – whose name, appropriately, was Alan Cash. From Nicosia we drove erratically to Limassol, the least fashionable part of the island where the station was based, taking in a number of bars and coffee shops and ending up at *Maxim*'s cabaret.

I was finally dropped off at a modest hotel on the sea front. Next morning, as I was queasily facing a pair of fried eggs cooked in olive oil, the Cypriot waiter serving me suddenly seized a large trident leaning by the door, hurled it into the harbour and came back into the restaurant with an octopus writhing on its prongs.

As a temporary bachelor I was a welcome addition to the unmarried members of the staff. My first night in Cyprus rather set the pattern until Moyra finally arrived by boat from England and helped to restore my health.

Clandestine Road

The Near East Arab Broadcasting Station (*Sharq al Adna* in Arabic) was a collection of Nissen army huts on a scrubby slope near the village of Polymedia overlooking Limassol.

Moyra and I lived in a mud brick house in a village a few miles away, rented from the local policeman. To modernise it to Western tastes, Andreas the policeman had nailed up a large oil drum to the back wall to serve as a shower, and each morning a tiny old woman, dressed all in black, would haul up buckets of icy cold water from a deep garden well, climb up a wooden ladder and fill the drum. We had to take our freezing morning shower in swimsuits as the villagers would line up outside the garden for the occasion to watch our strange ritual and hear our screams.

The garden also contained a big, bee-hive shaped mud oven. You threw in sticks and brushwood, closed the door and built up a tremendous heat which cooked a tough Cyprus leg of lamb to perfection. The only problem was that once smoke was observed, villagers, exercising apparently an ancient right, would appear with pieces of meat of all shapes and sizes, small birds, chickens and half turkeys, for roasting. After the oven door had been repeatedly opened the heat would escape, and everything would have to be taken out and the oven lit all over again.

The station broadcast in Arabic to the Arab world from Cyprus over what was then the most powerful medium-wave transmitter in the Middle East. It had a far larger audience than the BBC overseas services which in those days broadcast, indistinctly, only on short wave. We could also take a stronger pro-British political slant than the BBC could afford to. The objectives of British policy were to protect Britain's strategic and oil interests in the Middle East and its lines of communication. This meant opposition to Arab and Iranian nationalism which supported nationalisation of Western oil interests and opposed British military power in the region.

NEABS had originally been an English language British forces radio station in Palestine during the Second World War. After the war, it was taken over by the Special Political Activities section of the SIS, whose role was to provide the cover for a clandestine propaganda

Arabic radio station with the Foreign Office responsible for political guidance. The millions of pounds of funding for the station came out of MI6's budget from the secret vote. The British government somewhat unconvincingly denied any association with the station, which had to be transferred to Cyprus after the creation of Israel.

The supposed advantage to this curious piece of British deception was that the NEABS had freedom to express views without accountability by the government. When questions were raised in Parliament the government denied association, asserting, improbably, that the broadcasting station was a private company registered in Cyprus to promote cultural and information exchange in the Near East.

None of our listeners were fooled by this, but its covert role did not stop the station from being one of the most successful in the region – due in part to a first-class drama and music programme supplied by the station's largely Palestinian Arab staff. The 150 or so Arabs on the staff were a respectable, sober, hard-working group, mostly married with children. The small British expatriate staff of administrators, technicians and journalists were a racier lot altogether, whose goings-on constantly amazed their Arab colleagues.

Hangover

In those stark, austere, post-war days, the NEABS was a hangover, in more ways than one, from the carefree, outrageous intelligence world of the Second World War. Its clandestine propaganda role was already out of date. However, this was not immediately apparent to the British government, nor to the British staff who would broadcast to their Arab listeners on their need to accept Britain's role as nanny in the Middle East.

After an all-day picnic of kebab, ouzo, wine and beer aboard the station's boat in the blazing Mediterranean sun, we would continue the party at editor Derek Chudleigh's house until midnight, when it was time to drive to the station and prepare the dawn news bulletin. Occasionally the Arab news shift that arrived at dawn to translate the bulletin into Arabic would find a blank sheet of paper in his typewriter. But usually, against all the odds, there was a fairly professional news bulletin ready to go.

Not only the Arab staff, but the respectable Cypriot business community of Limassol, were deeply shocked by the *louche* behaviour of some of the British contingent. One senior member of the staff was sent back to England after mistaking, in the middle of a cocktail

party, the drawing-room grate for a urinal in a rather grand Cypriot
house where he was being entertained by Limassol society.

Then there was the case of a very large and very gentle British
member of staff. He was normally shy and sober, but from time to
time he would get sensationally drunk and was liable to cause spectacular scenes in public. On one occasion, he seized a street trader's
mobile kebab stand, a frail affair with a charcoal stove supported by
two bicycle wheels, and raced with it through the town with sausages
and sparks flying, pursued by the angry stall owner and the local
dogs.

One station scandal was related not to drink but to espionage.
Since the British staff had to interpret British policy to the Arab
world, we were given access to secret Foreign Office Intels (intelligence telegrams) sent over on diplomatic radio from London.
Frequent visits by a British member of the staff to Nicosia aroused suspicion. He was followed and it was eventually discovered that he was
regularly passing on the secrets of British policy in the Middle East,
such as they were, to the Israeli Consul General in Cyprus.

Propaganda War

Like the Colonial authorities, the British staff of NEABS seemed
totally unaware of the political volcano they were all sitting on in
Cyprus. Except for the occasional social blunder in our local relations, there was little contact with Cyprus society, and our vision was
focused across the sea on the Arab World. Indeed, I remember one
talk broadcast to the Arabs and written by the editor which spoke of
pictures of the Royal Family which adorned the walls of most Cypriot
village homes. Hardly a regular visitor to such places, he had somehow missed the point that it was the Greek Royal Family and not
ours that was always displayed.

There was considerable shock, therefore, when in 1955 General
George Grivas and his gunmen, aboard the good ship *St George*,
landed in Cyprus. Advocating insurrection and union with Greece,
he began a campaign of terror on the island and put an end to our
innocence.

But before that happened, and within months of my arrival,
Cyprus was already ceasing to be a forgotten colonial outpost.
Instead, it was being transformed to play a central role in what
became Britain's disastrous Middle East strategy for the 1950s. Anti-
British riots in Egypt followed by the overthrow of King Farouk and
the rise of President Gamal Abdel Nasser made Britain's position in

Suez untenable. In 1952 Britain's joint armed forces headquarters in
Suez was moved to Cyprus and with it the political control – the
British Middle East Office.

At the same time, the emergence of Nasser fired up the forces of
Arab nationalism. This began to make things distinctly uncomfort-
able for Britain throughout the Arab world. Meanwhile, President
Nasser increasingly became an obsession of the British government,
and finally succeeded in driving its future Prime Minister Anthony
Eden out of his mind.

The aspect of all these changes that most directly affected our
little band in Limassol was the emergence of a formidable new rival
radio station in the Arab propaganda war – *Sawt el Arab* ('The Voice
of the Arabs'). It was one of Nasser's first creations in his bid for leadership of the Middle East and became a major problem for Britain in
its efforts to maintain its influence in the region.

Until the Nasser revolution, our radio station had had no real
regional rivals. With our own orchestra, drama group and studios in
Beirut we were far more professional and sophisticated than the
other national radio stations in the Arab world. Soon, however, 'The
Voice of the Arabs' was dominating the air waves of the region, its
increasingly large transmitters broadcasting a torrent of anti-British
and anti-Israeli invective which was enthusiastically received by many
of its listeners.

Nowhere was it more successful in stirring up trouble than in that
cosy little pocket of British influence in the Arab World, the
Hashemite Kingdom of Jordan, where half the population were bitter
refugees from the former British Mandate of Palestine. In a vain
attempt to counter this, NEABS decided to establish a bureau in the
Jordanian capital Amman, and sent me there to set it up and to be its
correspondent.

MG

NEABS's idea was to have a British staffer on what we quaintly called
'The Mainland' to co-ordinate the coverage of our Arab stringers in
the capitals of the Arab world. Since Jordan had become a major
problem, it was decided to set up our chief bureau in Amman.

Until then, Moyra and I had not owned more than a bicycle. But I
decided that with the new job, I needed a car. I was looking for something sensible for desert travel, when I passed a showroom in Nicosia
and beheld a brand new two-seater TD MG in the window. It was ivory
with green leather upholstery and I was instantly in love. The price

seemed outrageous – £640 (I recently saw the same model for sale in London for £28,000). My employers thought my choice thoroughly frivolous. However, I managed to persuade the local manager of Barclays Bank to lend me the money and a few days later I arrived back from the broadcasting station to find the MG, looking stunning, standing in a green field opposite our cottage.

It was impractical, under-powered and gave the impression of great speed when travelling at 50 miles per hour. The petrol pump, housed under the back axle, frequently stopped working and had to be hit sharply with the winding handle. But it was a sensational first in Amman and remains the only car I have truly cared for.

2

Jordan

Desert Kingdom

In the early Spring of 1953, Moyra and I sailed to Beirut from Cyprus, then drove over the mountains to Damascus and across the Syrian desert to Amman with what little baggage a TD MG would carry. Crossing into Jordan through the rather sinister and depressing frontier town of Deraa, where TE Lawrence was notoriously raped by the Turkish commander, was to enter another world.

It was the same bit of basalt desert where a line had been drawn in the 1920s by Winston Churchill separating British and French influence in that benighted chunk of the Ottoman Empire. The Syrian side of the frontier was staffed with suspicious, surly, unshaven customs and security men looking for trouble and bribes.

On the Jordan side of the customs post there was a table covered with a British Army blanket, Arab Legion troops in British battle dress, red and white keffiyehs, mugs of tea and a friendly welcome. Glubb Pasha – General John Bagot Glubb – ran the Army, a 17-year-old King Hussein was still at Sandhurst, and the Hashemite Kingdom of Jordan seemed as British as Buckingham Palace.

Transjordan had been created by Britain after the First World War, and handed over to the rule of the Hashemite Prince Abdullah, whose family had been driven out of Saudi Arabia by King Ibn Saud. In 1948, in the fighting during the creation of Israel, the Arab Legion seized the West Bank of Palestine and the old city of Jerusalem. Transjordan then annexed the region and changed the Kingdom's name to Jordan. In 1967 Israel gained control of the West Bank, and Jordan reverted to its Transjordanian frontiers.

However, when we arrived, Jordan, like Cyprus, was about to let go of Nanny's hand – and enter a harsher, meaner world in which, against all odds, it has somehow managed to survive. The three years I spent there saw the abrupt end of that special relationship with the United Kingdom, leaving a country created by Britain, with no real identity or justification for its existence, to live on its wits and the resourcefulness of its King.

Amman, then and now

Amman was a ramshackle, shabby little town in those days, the capital of a country whose heavy industry consisted of a cement factory and a cigarette plant and whose largest employer was the *Jaysh al-Arabi*, the Arab Legion.

It had seen better days. Around 60 BC it had been known as Philadelphia, a Roman market town and one of the ten thriving cities of the Decapolis, a Roman confederacy which included Damascus. A large Roman amphitheatre survives next to the Philadelphia Hotel, which was one of only two of Amman's hotels deemed suitable for Westerners. It was known to the foreign community as the 'Filthydelphia', and represented the last word in naughty, sophisticated Amman nightlife. Hungarian and East German cabaret girls, on a circuit which usually included Cyprus, Baghdad and Basra and ended up at the Gordan Cabaret in Khartoum, would perform the Sailor's Hornpipe, a Scottish Reel and a Dance Oriental.

At one point, the amphitheatre made a brief return to its more barbaric days when the Jordanian authorities began, as a warning to others, to hold public executions of Arabs accused of spying for Israel. A temporary gallows was erected at the entrance to the auditorium and the victim was made to stand on a plank supported by the tailboards of two trucks which then drove away in opposite directions. The spectacle, however, had a distressing effect on guests at the Philadelphia, out on an early morning stroll, and was abandoned in the interests of Jordan's tourist industry.

By the start of the twentieth century, in Ottoman times, Amman had been reduced to little more than a village. It was policed, it was said, solely by a Turkish corporal and a private who were so feared that the townspeople would close their shutters when the two of them walked through the streets.

In the 1920s, Amman was chosen to be the capital of Transjordan by Hussein's grandfather Emir Abdullah after the Hashemites had been chased out of the Hejaz by the Saudis. During the 1948 war, which saw the creation of Israel, the population of Jordan more than doubled with the flood of Palestinian refugees, and when we arrived, a large proportion of the population was living in tents – either the black tents of the Bedouin tribes or the canvas tents of the United Nations sheltering hundreds of thousands of refugees.

By the 1950s, Amman comprised one bookshop, a few banks, a souk and a mosque. It was a dusty desert town, built along a dried-up river bed and surrounded by seven steep, brown hills, where Bedouin with their camels would come to barter goods. One hill, Jebel el-Hashimiya, had been taken over entirely by the Hashemite royal family, but the British had seen to it that the British Ambassador's residence was planted right inside the palace ground – just a stroll away from the royal palaces.

Our house was on top of another of Amman's hills, Jebel Hussein. It was reached by a desert track which, in winter, turned into mud, and behind it was a huge, bleak, United Nations administered tented encampment where thousands of Palestinian refugees alternately baked or froze. Our next door neighbour was a princess, an aunt of King Hussein. During the long, dry summers a water cart would arrive regularly to irrigate her high-walled garden where refugees would line up with cans to catch the drips from the leaky hosepipe. An English nanny in charge of Hussein's little brother Hassan would from time to time bring Hassan to visit the Princess. They would then drop in for a cup of tea with my wife and daughter Jennifer who was born shortly after we arrived.

Jennifer was looked after by a teenage Kurdish refugee girl, Hanifee, who wore billowy skirts, Kurdish trousers and had long, red hair in plaits down to her waist. Hanifee lived in a tent below our house with her father, his two wives and several children. She had a fiery temper and a deep Kurdish contempt for all Arabs and used to hurl insults at any unfortunate tradesman or workman who came to the house.

In the summer from our pink stone house you could see right over the pale brown hills to the surrounding desert as the sunset brought with it delicious cooling breezes after the heat of the day. From the back of the house, you could see in the far distance the light from the tomb of Abdullah, shot dead in the Al Aqsa Mosque in Jerusalem in 1951 as his sixteen-year-old grandson Hussein stood by his side. Winters on Jebel Hussein could be dismally cold, wet and raw, even if you lived in a house. But for a month or so before the desert summer arrived, the barren hills of Jordan were miraculously transformed with carpets of wild flowers, cyclamen, anemones and black tulips.

Now, the hills and desert that stretched towards the horizon have been engulfed with houses, hotels, offices and highways. Sprawling suburbs obliterate the Circassian villages and the black tent sites of the Bedouins that surrounded the town.

Amman today is a testimony to the political and economic stability created, against all odds, by King Hussein and his instinct for survival. In the midst of a volatile and highly unstable Arab world, Amman has attracted the confidence and capital to create a modern Middle Eastern city, clean, efficient and respectable – and exceedingly dull.

The Little King

We arrived in Amman a couple of months before Hussein was brought back from Sandhurst on reaching his eighteenth birthday to take over the throne. His father King Talal had become an incurable schizophrenic. At times, he became dangerous and violent and had to be restrained from attacking his wife, Queen Zain. Occasionally, he escaped his handlers in the palace to make sorties into town and was once involved in a shooting incident outside the post office.

Hussein's elder brother Muhammad seems to have inherited his father's condition. On one occasion he arrived back at Amman airport, scrambled up the tail of the aeroplane armed with a sten gun and had to be coaxed down. Muhammad has been barred from succession, with his brother, Hassan, seven years his junior, as Crown Prince.

Talal, before schizophrenia took over, was a quiet, likeable character. But his father Abdullah despised his son, regarding him as a weakling, and his cruel treatment may have contributed to Talal's mental breakdown. He kept Talal and Zain in such poverty that they came to rely upon secret handouts from the British Embassy, and the British minister even had to lend them the money for the hire purchase of a refrigerator for their palace.

King Hussein tells in his autobiography how his baby sister died of pneumonia during a cold winter in Amman because his parents could not afford proper heating. How they had to sell his bicycle, a present from his cousin the future King Feisal of Iraq, to pay the bills. But as Hussein grew up Abdullah began to see him as the son he had always wanted. Hussein adored him and, paradoxically, it was witnessing Abdullah's horrifying assassination that appears to have given his grandson his sense of fatalism and indifference to death.

The first time I met Hussein was shortly after his return from Sandhurst and his inauguration. I was having a drink one evening during Ramadan at the Royal Jordanian Automobile Club with a government minister, Anwar Nuseibeh, who always broke his day-long fast with a large scotch and soda! Hussein walked into the club, a tiny, erect figure with the voice of a giant, straight out of the Royal Military Academy, and, as he was introduced to the members, stood to attention with his thumbs down the seams of his trousers, gave us a big smile and called each of us 'Sir'.

The Kingdom Hussein inherited was almost totally dependent on British subsidies. The British residency was planted right inside the palace grounds a short stroll from the Basman Palace, an RAF station was across the valley next to Amman airport and Glubb and his British officers were in charge of the Army and security. All of this was to be transformed by the polite young Sandhurst cadet who was soon to prove that he had a mind of his own.

The King and the Pasha

The Kingdom of Jordan was ringed with enemies. Saudi Arabia, Syria and Egypt were seeking to destroy it, and it was at war with Israel with 400 miles of frontier to defend. Despite this, there was a strangely carefree, frivolous, Ruritanian atmosphere about Amman. The King had just discovered sex, fast cars and planes, and go-karting around the airport runway. There was endless palace gossip about Hussein's latest affairs, and the doings of his wicked uncle, the queen's brother Sharif Nasser, who had made a fortune in the hashish trade.

It was Major Ali Abu Nuwar who is credited with having been the first to introduce Hussein to the pleasures of sex when Hussein, still a Sandhurst cadet, visited Paris where Nuwar was the Jordanian military attaché. As soon as he came to the throne, Hussein brought Nuwar back to the Palace, later sacked Glubb, and unwisely gave Nuwar his job.

Poor Glubb, a shy, retiring man, and a contemporary of Hussein's grandfather Abdullah, was totally out of his depth in such matters. Shortly before Hussein's Paris adventures Glubb recounts in his book, *A Soldier with the Arabs,* how he visited the king at Harrow, when he was 16, and took him for an out-of-school treat:

I took the Amir out for the afternoon. We went to the Battersea Festival Gardens, but he was not amused. He did not want to go on the merry-go-rounds or the scenic railway. I must have misunderstood his age-group, or his early introduction to public affairs in such tragic circumstances had sobered him prematurely. On the return journey, we paid a visit to Fortnum and Mason. The Royal Chamberlain in Amman had been unaware that English public school boys had tuck boxes. We repaired the omission.

Glubb had treated Hussein as a child. But Ali Abu Nuwar, the scheming military attaché in Paris, got it right! Glubb, who commanded the Arab Legion for 26 years, was only really at home with his Bedouin troops. The Glubbs were a totally old-fashioned English product, modest, self-effacing and church-going, taking no part in the social life of Amman.

Shortly after we arrived in Jordan, we attended the annual Arab Legion Day Parade – a colourful march-past in the desert of camel patrols, slightly outdated armoured cars and the Legion pipe band. Moyra found herself standing among the spectators next to a rather dowdy, middle-aged Englishwoman. 'What do you do in Amman?' Moyra enquired. 'Oh, my husband works for the Arab Legion' came the reply. She was, of course, Lady Glubb.

Although the mildest looking of men (an impression enhanced by the fact that part of his chin had been shot away in the First World War), Glubb was in fact a formidable personality, steeped in the lore of the desert. He came to Transjordan in 1930 from Iraq, where he had put an end to desert raiding by Bedouin tribes.

Performing a similar role in Transjordan, he took over a small Arab Legion force of camel-mounted desert police and by employing the tribesmen themselves to police their own deserts ended raiding without firing a shot. Glubb knew personally every man and his family in his desert police force. In 1939 he assumed command from another British officer, Colonel Peake Pasha, of the Legion which was only about a thousand strong. By 1941, Transjordan, the sole ally of Britain in the region, was surrounded by enemies. Syria and Lebanon were pro-Axis and, after a coup, Iraq declared war on Britain.

A tiny, mobile force of the Arab Legion nevertheless invaded Iraq and crossed 500 miles of desert to help relieve the RAF base at Habbaniya. The Legion then marched with the British Army into Syria and helped defeat the Vichy French. Throughout the war, as Glubb recounts, his army developed an extraordinary spirit of comradeship with the British Army. In 1948, the Arab Legion occupied the West Bank of Palestine and was the only Arab Army to withstand the forces of Israel.

By the time that we arrived in Jordan in 1953, the Arab Legion had grown to a force of 23,000. But Glubb still tried to run it as a family affair. I remember one evening, at a time of great tension in Amman after a new round of pro-Nasser riots, I was having a drink with the

Legion's adjutant, Colonel Ken Heish, when the phone rang. 'What was that all about?' I asked Ken, sensing a story, after he had had a longish call with Glubb. 'Oh,' said Ken, 'apparently some shorts for the army's football team have gone missing and the Pasha wants to know what's happened to them!'

Glubb was never really on the same wavelength as the large corps of British officers, some from rather smart regiments, seconded from the Army or on contract as 'hired assassins', who had been thrust upon him as the Legion grew into a modern army. These officers and their families were mostly stationed in Zerqa, but joined in the hectic social life of Amman's foreign community who, as well as the rounds of dances and parties staged elaborate, amateur dramatic performances at Jerash and in the palace grounds, and organised picnics on the Dead Sea and expeditions to Aqaba and Petra.

The RAF at Amman airport in contrast lived rather sheltered lives, sticking to their swimming pool and messes and rarely venturing outside their perimeter fence. Some daring young aircraftmen did discover the attractions of the Greek Bar, a sleazy café near the souk whose owner could procure some fairly basic female company. However, the wife of the RAF commanding officer determined to try to save these young men from sin by providing alternative attractions. Once a week she used to round up the younger matrons of the British community, including Moyra, for an evening of wholesome Scottish dancing at the RAF station – while we husbands, with little else to do, usually ended up at the Greek Bar.

Having exhausted the delights of Amman, you could strike out into the desert and lunch with a Bedouin tribe whose elders could still recall the uprising against the Turks, and even Lawrence of Arabia. The Bedouins whom I met never thought a great deal of Lawrence or his role in the war. But they did remember him enviously as the British agent with bags and bags of gold.

The Bedouins would provide a *mencef* of camel, sheep or goat served on a huge brass tray with rice. The host, without fail, would hand you the least appealing piece of meat which you would squash up with some soggy rice and swallow as quickly as you could.

I was once at a *mencef* provided by the Beni Sakhr tribe with Sir Patrick Coghill, the then head of security in Jordan. Coghill marched up to the tray, made a pellet of a small quantity of rice, popped it in his mouth and then strode off to wash his hands. I asked him how he could get away with such a cavalier performance. 'When I was a very young ADC,' he said, 'I was invited to lunch with a Greek general. We were each served with a white soup plate containing about two dozen sheep's eyeballs rolling around like marbles. After that experience I felt I had done my duty to my monarch and since then I have refused to eat anything I don't want.'

There was even a British commander of a Jordanian naval flotilla – Marine Major Geoffrey Douglas, known as the Dead Sea Lord. He commanded a flotilla of small gunboats on the Dead Sea – the Dead Sea Fleet. He used to train his sailors to become accustomed to underwater warfare by organising games with big, lead-weighted playing cards on the sea bed. I waited in vain for a clash with Israeli patrol boats and had already prepared the headline 'Dead Sea Lord in Naval Battle a Thousand Feet Below Sea Level'.

Seducing the King

Nobody gave King Hussein, or Jordan, much of a chance of survival with half the population, mostly Palestinians, hostile and his neighbours moving in for the kill. But the monarchy was all that gave Jordan any sense of identity and so, inevitably, there was rivalry among the diplomatic community to have someone in place to influence the king. Glubb, who had had a close relationship with King Abdullah, was two generations too old. Britain had to find someone, and the unlikely candidate the Foreign Office posted to Amman to befriend the King was a young embassy third secretary with absolutely nothing in common with Hussein. He was Johnny Graham, a charming, serious, rather intellectual upper-class Scot, who later became ambassador to Saudi Arabia, and whose only vice, as far as is known, was playing his bagpipes in the bath.

The American choice, rather more suitable, was John Dayton, a young CIA man with a low clerical rank in the US Embassy. Dayton, by the standards of the 1950s, was a swinger. He had a flat in downtown Amman with his sitting room painted entirely in black and the latest hi-fi equipment that technology could then provide. He even went off on a brief holiday to the States and came back with an extremely pretty young Southern wife who, envious cynics said, was chosen to catch the eye of the king.

However the British all the time, had had the ideal candidate for the job, but were too rigid and snobbish to employ him. He was an RAF Squadron Leader, Jock Dalgleish, second-in-command to the Arab Legion Air Force and the king's best friend. Dalgleish, who was in Jerusalem on the day Abdullah was assassinated, told a shaken Hussein 'I'll look after you', swept him up and flew him back to Amman.

Dalgleish became Hussein's hero when he taught the king how to fly, and later when he saved his life by outmanoeuvring two Syrian fighter aircraft when they tried to force the king's plane to crash in the desert. Hussein loved being accepted into the Dalgleish's broad Scots, middle-class family life, and sharing cups of tea and sandwiches in the kitchen with them and their children. However, instead of exploiting the relationship, the king's friendship with the Dalgleish family severely miffed the British Embassy. When Dalgleish's tour came to an end, the British unwisely refused Hussein's request to extend it – and lived to regret their decision.

Several years later, after Moscow had established diplomatic relations with Amman, the KGB also had a crack at getting in with the king. For their honeytrap operation they posted the Petrovskis to Amman – a stylish, young Russian couple who spoke good English and, compared with their stodgy Soviet embassy counterparts, looked like visitors from another planet. Whether King Hussein took the bait – the slim blonde Olga Petrovski – was never recorded. But it was clear he already suspected their motives, when a British intelligence officer went to warn him about what the Russians were up to.

The Petrovskis, suspiciously with plenty of money to spend, had no restraints on their social life and soon became a popular couple with the foreign community. They said they had a child in Moscow and appeared particularly fond of their German shepherd dog which guarded their house. They got to know the king, and used to spend weekends in Aqaba where Hussein regularly went water ski-ing. After a brief trip back to the Soviet Union, Olga Petrovski, it was observed, returned as an accomplished water-skier.

In one melodramatic moment of the Cold War, the MI6 man who had originally warned the king, spotted Olga alone, sunbathing on a raft. It was an ideal opportunity for an unbugged conversation so he swam out to her and offered the KGB couple political asylum if they agreed to defect. But she refused, explaining that she did not know what would happen to her son if she defected to the West.

No one knows for certain what happened next, but it was believed that the Soviet Ambassador, increasingly jealous of the Petrovskis and their lifestyle, warned Moscow that they were being seduced by Western life and had become a security risk. Petrovski was suddenly summoned to Beirut, the KGB regional headquarters, sent to Damascus and put on an Aeroflot plane for Moscow. A distraught Olga Petrovski called on her Western friends to say goodbye, claiming that her husband had had to flee because of a British intelligence plot to kill him. The next day a Soviet embassy limousine picked her

up and drove her to Damascus to catch the next flight out. The dog
was shot.

Border Warfare

One of the main tasks of my Jordan assignment was to cover the turbulent Jordan–Israeli frontier, and it was the progressively worsening
frontier situation that led directly to the collapse of British suzerainty
in Jordan.

Whenever there was a serious frontier clash, I had to dash over to
the West Bank, then part of Jordan, and try to file my account of the
event before the Israeli propaganda machine went into action with its
version of the bloodshed. To aid me in this, I had a useful source
right inside Glubb's headquarters in Amman – Moyra had taken a job
working for the intelligence section of the Arab Legion, which plot-
ted the course of border incursions and tried to predict the location
of the next Israeli attack.

Most incidents took place along the Palestinian frontier villages
overlooking the thin waist of Israel and the Mediterranean. The villagers in the rocky foothills had to watch their orange and olive
groves in the fields beyond the armistice lines being harvested by
Israeli farmers. Infiltration and raiding across the demarcation lines
by the villagers were met with the traditional policy of massive
reprisals by the Israeli Army.

The Arab Legion was too weak to protect the entire frontier from
Israeli night attacks and the incidents I covered were depressingly
repetitive. The Israeli forces, often Arabic-speaking Druze contingents, would surround a small village, blow up the houses with the
villagers inside, mine the access road and set up an ambush for Arab
Legion troops coming to the rescue.

On one occasion, I came upon an engagement in which Arab
Legion forces became surrounded by the Israelis and were trying to
extricate themselves. 'What are you going to do now, Sir?' I asked
Glubb, who happened to be on the spot, bullets whizzing around
him. Glubb, the most self-effacing and courteous of men, looked at
me calmly with his pale blue eyes. 'I don't know, Beeston,' he replied
softly. 'What do you suggest?' Since the rank of subaltern was the
highest I ever reached in the Army, I decided to retire quietly without
giving him the benefit of my advice.

One of the worst incidents I reported was in October 1953 when
the Israelis attacked the village of Qibya, levelled it to the ground and
killed 66 villagers, mainly women and children. The man responsible

was Ariel Sharon, then a 25-year-old Israeli Defence Force Major. Sharon was to gain further international notoriety as defence minister for his role in the 1982 invasion of Lebanon and the Shatila refugee camp massacre. In response to Arab infiltrations and terrorist attacks, Sharon had raised a ruthless commando unit, the 101st special forces. He trained it to respond tenfold, attacking Jordanian frontier villages regardless of civilian casualties, and Qibya was one of his first operations.

The Qibya massacre proved a fatal moment for Glubb. Riots broke out in Amman, Jerusalem, Nablus and Jericho, fuelled by President Nasser's 'Voice of the Arabs' broadcasts. Glubb and the British were the target for failing to protect the frontier, and this became the pattern for the next two years.

President Nasser was bent on destroying both British influence in Jordan and the Hashemite monarchy, and the more lies and distortions that the 'Voice of the Arabs' broadcast, the more popular it and Nasser became. On one occasion I travelled with a Palestinian past peaceful refugee camps in the Jordan Valley where Egyptian broadcasts were claiming refugees were rioting and blocking the road. 'How how can you listen to "The Voice of the Arabs" when you see what they say is not true?' I asked the Palestinian. 'Because what they broadcast is what we like to hear,' he replied.

Glubb, growing increasingly concerned about Nasser's propaganda, once asked me why my radio station could not counter it. I replied that we could only broadcast true accounts of what was happening in the hope that our listeners would trust us – I discovered that even educated Arabs who, on one level, believed most of what we and the BBC had to say, also fervently listened to Cairo for what they liked to hear.

Almost a Cinder

After Qibya, Jordan became an increasingly more volatile and unfriendly place in which to live. The last straw came in late 1955 when Britain persuaded Jordan to join the new and ill-fated Baghdad Pact, a defensive alliance involving Turkey, Iraq, Pakistan and Iran.

Field Marshal Sir Gerald Templer, Chief of the Imperial General Staff, was sent to Amman to sell the idea. King Hussein fell for it, largely because of British promises to provide a squadron of *Vampire* jets for his air force and increased subsidies for his army. However, Egypt denounced the pact as a British pro-Israeli plot, and 'The Voice of the Arabs' brought more rioters than ever out into the streets.

The riots, which had spread throughout Jordan, reached their climax on 8 January 1956. I was in my bureau, opposite the Prime Minister's office and the US Aid headquarters, when thousands of rioters erupted from downtown Amman and started looting and setting fire to buildings.

I watched uneasily as the mob drew closer, but as our bureau was built into the hillside behind large iron gates and a long, steep flight of stone steps, it was by then too late to escape. Two fire engines which came to put out the fires were attacked and set ablaze. The rioters were battering at the gates when I managed to get a call through to Glubb. 'I am afraid, Beeston, there is nothing I can do to help you unless the Government authorises the use of the Army,' he said in a calm, matter-of-fact voice, and put down the receiver.

I was clearly a target for these anti-British riots and had no escape or hiding place. Our Syrian landlord, a wealthy, miserly man lived next to the office but his door was bolted.

Apart from my radio job I was also stringing for Associated Press. Since I had nowhere to go, I thought I might as well telephone the story of the Amman riots through to AP in Damascus, and was doing so when the rioters burst through the gates, armed with flaming torches.

It looked like the end of a pleasant career, when suddenly I heard the shrill, hysterical ululating shrieks of women outside my door. I opened it and found on top of the steps the landlord's two teenage daughters, sent out by their father to save his property, screaming and beating their naked breasts.

Fortunately for me, the sight was too much for the Moslem demonstrators who, deeply shocked by the sight of the bare-breasted girls, turned tail, dashed down the stairs, and instead ransacked the deserted US Aid offices opposite and set fire to the Department of Agriculture.

Glubb later described receiving a series of frantic phone calls like my own, but had to delay sending in the troops until he had specific authorisation. Finally, the Jordanian Prime Minister Samir Pasha came on the line. 'The crowd is getting dangerous,' he said. 'They are burning the town. Call the army at once.'

'Do you order the troops to open fire if necessary?' asked Glubb. 'Yes, yes. Disperse them at once. Open fire, they will burn the city down.'

Later that evening I visited the home of an Arab Legion officer whose house overlooked my bureau and whose family had witnessed the riot. While I was enjoying a whisky, and the fact I was still alive, my host's small son gave me a disappointed look. 'Daddy,' he complained, 'you said you thought Mr Beeston had been burned to a cinder.'

Although Glubb saved the capital he was made a scapegoat, and his unpopularity was blamed for the riots. Hussein dropped the Baghdad Pact like a hot potato and six weeks later sacked Glubb. Summoned to the prime minister's office, Samir Pasha told him that 'His Majesty came here this morning and said he thinks it is time you had a rest. Can you leave in two hours?'

'No sir, I cannot,' Glubb replied. 'I have lived here for 26 years. Almost all my worldly possessions are here, to say nothing of my wife and children.'

Finally he was given until 7 o'clock the following morning to depart – with one suitcase of belongings each. Returning home he recounts his wife saying 'Hello dear, how nice, you are back earlier than usual. Were things slack today at the office?'

'My dear,' replied Glubb, 'the king has dismissed me. We leave Jordan at 7 o'clock tomorrow morning – and we shall never come back.'

'Well, have some tea now,' she said, 'then I'll put the children to bed and we'll pack all night.'

Their departure from Amman airport, however, was delayed while a despatch rider left the palace with a present for Glubb – a silver framed, signed photograph of the king.

To ensure his own survival, with his kingdom in a state of nationalistic ferment, King Hussein was probably right to sack his army commander, but it was a bold move for the 21-year-old monarch. Concerned over the possibility of an army move against him, he cut off the phones of all the Legion's British officers and placed them under virtual house arrest. The night the Glubbs were packing, said Hussein later, cables piled up on his desk beseeching him to revoke the decision, including a personal cable from the British Prime Minister Sir Anthony Eden. At a midnight meeting the British Ambassador Sir Charles Duke, who had been in touch with Eden, warned Hussein that the consequences of the decision could be very serious 'to yourself, the monarchy and the whole future of Jordan.'

Hussein stuck to his guns, and as a result, the Anglo-Jordan treaty was revoked and the British officers were withdrawn. Hussein then appointed in Glubb's place the one man in the army whom Glubb had most strongly warned him against – Colonel Ali Abu Nuwar.

For a brief period, King Hussein was hailed as a hero by Arab nationalists and he began promoting, to the concern of his loyal Bedouin officers, Palestinian, pro-Nasser friends of Nuwar. But in his book, *Uneasy Lies The Head,* he admits that after the departure of Glubb the once efficient army began to deteriorate into 'differing factions, each with its own political beliefs', and a leftist Arab nationalist Suleiman Nabulsi had become prime minister.

In the spring of 1957, just a year after Glubb's expulsion, Hussein, after his brief period of popularity, was being denounced as an imperialist agent and the storm clouds were forming over Jordan. By this time I had become the *News Chronicle* correspondent based in Beirut, but the deteriorating political situation in Jordan drew myself and other members of the press corps back to Amman.

We were there in time to report one of the most dramatic events of King Hussein's stormy career. With enemies in the army and the government seeking his overthrow, Hussein and his relations began contacting mainly Bedouin loyal units in the army to warn them of the dangers of a plot against the king. He also learned that Abu Nuwar had been in close touch with the Syrian military. Every detail of the conspiracy had been planned ahead, and flags of a new Jordanian Republic were later found in Abu Nuwar's desk. Meanwhile, a number of loyal army officers had pretended to join the conspiracy and warned the king of the date of the planned coup in April. Fighting then broke out in Zerqa between the conspirators and the Bedouin units.

Just as Hussein summoned Abu Nuwar to his palace, a message came through that a Bedouin brigade at Zerqa, hearing rumours that the King was dead was on its way to the palace. Hussein then ordered Abu Nuwar, by this time a very frightened man, to accompany him as he drove to Zerqa. Unfortunately for Abu Nuwar, they ran into a truckload of armed troops, who were firing into the air and shouting 'We are your men!' and on sighting General Abu Nuwar shouted 'kill him, there is the traitor!' With difficulty, Hussein rescued his commander-in-chief and sent him back to Amman.

There was still fighting in Zerqa when Hussein arrived. He was told that the Bedouin brigade had been paraded and ordered to leave immediately, on a long march, without their weapons, but the suspicious brigade had broken into the ammunition depot and attacked the officers they suspected of plotting a coup. Order was finally restored and Hussein drove back to the palace, where he found Abu Nuwar under arrest in Hussein's study.

Abu Nuwar, now 'a whining man, tears streaming down his face, fearful for his life,' begged Hussein to save him. 'I could not bring myself to put him to death. I was so tired, so sick with shame for my fellow human beings, I could not do it', the King said later.

Glubb was proven right, and the next day his successor was allowed to leave for Damascus – from where he had been taking orders all along.

Death of a Radio Station

Glubb's abrupt departure marked the end of an era for Britain in the Middle East. It also infuriated the Anthony Eden who accused Hussein of dismissing Glubb 'like a pilfering servant'. Eden's hatred, however, was concentrated on Nasser, whom he really held responsible for undermining British influence in Jordan. Perhaps more than any other incident except Egypt's seizure of the Suez Canal, Glubb's dismissal fuelled Eden's growing obsession with Egypt's President, whom he exaggeratedly began to equate with Adolf Hitler, an evil dictator to be overthrown at all costs. It was this hysteria that led Britain later in the year to join with France and Israel in the ill-fated Suez War.

Under the Anglo-Egyptian treaty of 1936, Britain had reserved the right to keep troops in the Suez Canal zone to protect the Suez canal. But after the overthrow of King Farouk, Britain in 1954 agreed to withdraw its troops and completed the operation by June 1956. The following month President Nasser nationalised the Canal and France, Britain and Israel made a secret agreement for a joint attack on Egypt. But their forces had to withdraw ignominiously in the face of furious opposition to the invasion by the United States.

One of the many, although comparatively minor casualties of Eden's Suez madness was my employer, the Near East Arab Broadcasting Station. During the previous year or so the station, despite its MI6 control, had become the first Middle East Radio station to go commercial, and proved an immediate success throughout the Arab world – promoting soap and aspirin and soft drinks. The station's growing profits presented a weird bureaucratic problem for the Treasury and the Secret Service. With advertising money pouring in, it was discovered that there was no authorisation for MI6 to make or spend profits from its operations and no way of laundering the money earned by commercial radio.

However, soon after the civil servants had found a formula, the only British Secret Service operation to start showing a healthy profit suddenly collapsed.

The British government decided it wanted a hard-line propaganda station to back up its invasion, intimidate the Egyptians and call for the overthrow of President Nasser. It took over direct charge of NEABS, changed its name to 'The Voice of Britain', and appointed the gung-ho Suez psychological warfare chief Brigadier Bernard Fergusson (who was later to become Governor General to New Zealand) to overall charge.

This was too much for the station's long-suffering director Ralph Poston, a liberal, Establishment figure who had worked for the Foreign Office and Chatham House. In an emotional speech to the Arab Staff, Poston went on the air to announce the takeover: 'I want everybody to know how I and all the staff of *Sharq al Adna* disagree with this policy over Suez which has produced this disastrous situation,' he proclaimed. Fergusson arrived at NEABS shortly afterwards to discover that all the Arab staff had resigned. He angrily denounced Poston as a traitor, sent British troops to surround his home and placed Poston and his family under house arrest.

By this time, however, I had been posted to Beirut, where NEABS had transferred its orchestra and drama section, and it was from here that I viewed the build-up of the Suez War and the collapse of the radio station that employed me.

Sir Donald Maitland, a future ambassador to Libya was brought in to run the station. The future head of the Foreign Office Sir Patrick Wright and Dick Fyjis-Walker, future ambassador to Pakistan, were among a group of young Foreign Office diplomats brought in order to help out and to make broadcasts in Arabic. The foreign office contingent did their best to tone down some of the excesses of the short-tempered, red-faced brigadier. Some of his blood-curdling threats to Egypt that did go over the air included: 'you've seen what the paras can do by day, wait till you see what they can do by night!', and: 'how would you like to feel the cold steel of a British bayonet in your back?'

Despite Fergusson's efforts, calls for the overthrow of Nasser and threats of dire retribution against those who supported him appeared to have little effect. When the Suez war ended, NEABS was found to be past all resuscitation. The government closed the station for good, sacked the staff, and handed its powerful medium-wave transmitter over to the BBC.

Ralph Poston, disillusioned with his experience in the service of the British government, became a vicar in the Church of England. Towards the end of his life he made another dramatic change and embraced Islam.

3

Lebanon

Suez Madness

In the spring of 1956, Moyra and I moved into a modern block of flats overlooking the Mediterranean and Beirut's famous rocks, the Grottes aux Pigeons. There were few other buildings there then – a Lebanese café perched precariously on the cliff-side, and in the vicinity there were some shepherds looking after a few scruffy goats and sheep grazing on thorns and camel grass.

Shortly after we settled in, our second daughter Fiona was born at the American University of Beirut hospital and we began to enjoy life in the Lebanon. There could not have been a greater contrast than Amman and Beirut – the difference between an English maiden aunt and a French mistress.

In Amman, a packet of spaghetti was considered pretty exotic. In Beirut, the French influence was pervasive with pavement cafés, stylish women who did their shopping in Paris, a fabulous flower market, palm trees along the corniche, a downtown city and port of delightful old red-tiled Turkish houses and restaurants serving the most delicious French and Lebanese dishes. An Arab brothel area larger than Piccadilly Circus and Leicester Square featured girls with their names in neon lights and garish artists' impressions of their charms.

Lebanon was in a period of tremendous expansion and prosperity. It began after independence in 1943, but the boom really occurred after the creation of Israel in 1948 isolated the Palestinian ports and made Beirut the main port of entry to the Arab world. Banks and Western firms poured into the city to mop up the fabulous new oil riches of the Gulf. Hotels and night clubs sprang up to cater to the tastes of a flood of Gulf millionaires whose diet only a few years previously had been camel's milk and a handful of dates.

The Maronite Christians largely ran Lebanon. They were out for a good time and there was an atmosphere of arrogant optimism that they had got things exactly right. Although villages and countryside of Lebanon remained little changed from Ottoman days, in Beirut there was a flashy 'everything has its price' feel about the place - summed up by a joke of the time: 'a Lebanese and an Englishman are sitting in the foyer of Beirut's Hotel St Georges watching the exceedingly well-dressed, well-connected society women come and go. As each one passes the Lebanese estimates the price – this one five hundred Lebanese pounds, the next one a thousand. "How much would you say that one would charge?" asks the Englishman, as a particularly alluring woman passes by. "Good Heavens" exclaims the Lebanese, "Don't you know who that is. That's the wife of the president! She is very, very expensive."'

A *Time* magazine correspondent Wilton Wynn once gave me his reaction to the Beirut of those days: 'It is a lovely bright morning. You come out onto the steps of the St. Georges. There are the taxi drivers, the pimps, the street sellers all watching you – and you suddenly realise that everyone around you is minding your own business.'

The war clouds over Egypt seemed to have surprisingly little effect on Lebanon. The largely pro-Western Christians detested Nasser, and the Egyptian leader had yet to consolidate his fanatical following among the Moslems.

We were having a quiet meal in a café one evening after the outbreak of war, when a local radio broadcast live coverage of the RAF dropping bombs on the outskirts of Cairo. I thought we would be attacked by angry Lebanese, but everyone appeared very subdued, little realising, no doubt, that the might of Britain and France in the Arab world was just about to collapse.

Cut off from my radio station and with little to do, I contacted the *News Chronicle*. The newspaper's sympathetic and delightful foreign editor, Sylvain Mangeot, agreed that I should string for them during the Suez crisis and its aftermath. If I could get some good stories and establish my name in the paper, he would try to get me a job as a reporter in the newsroom when I returned to London. Fortunately, there was no shortage of stories and I did manage to achieve a couple of world scoops for the *Chronicle* – a record I found much harder to maintain once I came on the staff!

The most satisfactory scoop came just after the Suez War when the British and French, under American pressure, were being forced into an ignominious withdrawal. Nasser, having lost most of his diplomatic contacts with the West, used a prominent Christian Lebanese businessman and politician, Emile Bustani, as his unofficial roving ambassador and peacemaker. Bustani happened to be a friend of mine, and hearing one morning that he had just that moment returned from a visit to Cairo, I dashed round to his office. 'Did you see Nasser?' I asked Emile. 'I saw him last night,' he replied, 'and what did he say?' 'He spelled out the six conditions for reopening the Suez canal, ending the war and restoring relations with the West.' It was one of those rare occasions when you hear of a diplomatic break-through before the diplomats. So I wrote down the six conditions and filed the story which the *Chronicle* splashed.

At the end of the Suez crisis I flew back to London. I did not want to return to a domestic newsroom job, but fortunately, Sylvain offered me the job as the paper's Middle East correspondent based in Beirut. He then took me to lunch at his club to explain my new duties. He had been working late the previous night and suffered from a sleep-ing-sickness problem. After the first course he nodded off. When he awoke it was time for the afternoon editorial conference, so I never really did get my briefing.

Cadbury's Chronicle

I was delighted to join the staff of the *News Chronicle*, a much respected liberal daily newspaper with a healthy circulation of well over a million, whose first editor was Charles Dickens. But I did not realise at the time that the Suez War, which had brought about the collapse of my radio station, would also become one of the final nails in the coffin of the *Chronicle*. Despite its prestige and circulation and a devoted staff which included some of the best writers in Fleet Street, the *News Chronicle* had lost its soul and was a dying paper.

We had some great bylines – James Cameron, Vernon Bartlett, Willie Forrest, Ritchie Calder and Ian Trethowan, who became direc-tor-general of the BBC – and the *Chronicle* had become known as the 'newspaperman's newspaper' for the quality of its writing, its lively news coverage and its absence of any stultifying political ideology.

But the paper deserved better than the ownership of the Cadbury family and its chocolate millionaire chairman Laurence Cadbury. Cadbury was easily the least impressive of the Fleet Street propri-etors. Something of a Dickensian character himself, his one claim to fame was his stinginess – he would walk half a mile to save a penny on the bus which brought him to the office every day.

He took special pleasure from the fact that his staff were the worst paid in Fleet Street, and he shared none of the liberal views for which his paper was supposed to stand. He vetoed all efforts by the *Chronicle*'s editor Michael Curtis to try to save the paper, and finally sold out to the *Daily Mail* – the most right-wing daily at that time and the paper he most admired.

The paper's main financial problem was its low advertising revenue. Unlike the *Mail* and the *Telegraph,* its readership was largely the not so well-off lower-middle-class liberals, teachers and radical intellectuals, who had limited appeal to advertisers. Plans by Curtis to try to take the paper upmarket were opposed by the Cadbury family who wanted to sell rather than risk any of their fortune.

The Suez War was a catalyst. The *Chronicle,* like the other liberal and left-wing papers , the *Manchester Guardian, The Observer* and the *Daily Herald,* all took an anti-Eden stand. All heavily lost circulation. The *Chronicle* had expected its readers to support its opposition to the Anglo-French–Israeli invasion of Egypt, but it had misinterpreted their mood. Once British troops landed in Egypt many switched from liberalism to a fierce patriotism and the *Chronicle* lost over 40,000 readers at a stroke. It survived for nearly four more years, but never really recovered from Suez.

Colleagues

On joining the *Chronicle* I became part of a growing corps of foreign correspondents based in Beirut to cover the Middle East during the turbulent years of Suez and its aftermath. Lebanon was the only Arab country without censorship and with good communications, so inevitably Beirut became the listening post for the region, with the St. Georges and its bar its epicentre – a bazaar for the trading of information between diplomats, politicians, journalists and spies.

The correspondents were an interesting crowd, mostly in their late twenties and thirties. A close friend of ours was Joe Alex Morris of the *Los Angeles Times,* shot dead in 1978 covering the upheavals that led to the overthrow of the Shah of Persia. Another friend was Tom Streithorst, the madcap NBC correspondent whose last story was anchoring the TV coverage of his own heart transplant operation! There was United Press correspondent Larry Collins, who fell passionately in love with the wife of Lebanon's Druze leader and went on to write bestsellers including *Is Paris Burning.* David Holden was *The Times* Middle East correspondent, later murdered mysteriously near Cairo airport. There was also *The New York Times* veteran correspondent Sam Pope Brewer and the newly arrived correspondent for *The Observer* and *The Economist* – Kim Philby.

We met Kim shortly after he arrived in 1956 and he used to come with us on family picnics in the Lebanese mountains or drop round for a drink at our flat. He seemed a rather lonely, rumpled figure, with a heavily lined but warm and friendly face and piercing blue eyes. He was quintessentially English, relaxed and courteous, amusing – and this, combined with a rather painful stammer, made him pretty well irresistible to women. He could charm the birds out of the trees, one American friend remarked. But a far darker side to his personality was to emerge.

After we had known him for a year or so, we met him one day while we were Christmas shopping in Beirut's Bab Idriss. 'I have wonderful news, darlings' he said crossing the road. 'I want you to come and celebrate.'

He took us to his favourite hotel, the Normandie, a far more modest establishment than the St. Georges, and produced a telegram from England announcing the death of his wife Aileen. Seeing that we looked stunned, he explained that her death was 'a wonderful escape'. He said that she had been mentally unstable to the extent that at times she had inflicted wounds on herself and had not been well for years.

We later learned that Aileen, who came from a prosperous English county family, towards the end almost certainly knew of, and was haunted by Kim's life of treason, and had seriously taken to drink. In the last year of her life she had been reduced to doing domestic work for friends to help support herself and her four children.

During our drink at the Normandy, Kim announced that he was free to marry 'a wonderful American girl' he had known for some time. We assumed she was some young thing he had met, but soon discovered that it was Sam Brewer's wife Eleanor.

Kim was 45 at the time, Eleanor a couple of years younger. She was a rangy, steady-drinking American, who looked tough and sophisticated. Underneath she was in fact a romantic, and politically naive – and Philby broke her heart.

Shortly after our encounter we used to see Kim and Eleanor, dining out together and, like young lovers, wandering round the city hand in hand. For that period and for a little time after their marriage they seemed transformed, drinking far less and delighting in each other's company. But it was not to last.

Third Man

Kim Philby, of course, came to Lebanon with a suspicious 'Third Man' cloud over his head. But allegations that, while in the British

Secret Service, he had tipped off the Soviet agents Guy Burgess and Donald Maclean in time for them to defect had been officially denied by the British Prime Minister Harold Macmillan: 'I have no reason to conclude that Mr Philby has at any time betrayed the interests of this country, or to identify him with the so-called Third Man, if, indeed, there was one', Macmillan told parliament. Philby's forced resignation was a direct result of American pressure. Although there was no conclusive evidence of Philby's treachery, the CIA threatened to end collaboration with the British security services unless he was purged.

However, many of Philby's colleagues believed he was an innocent victim of an American witch-hunt and the SIS appealed to David Astor, owner of *The Observer*, to take Kim on. They assured Astor that Philby was not a Soviet agent, and that he had no longer any links with the British Secret Service. Both assertions turned out to be false. But Kim certainly fooled me, and probably his other press colleagues too.

I did not believe he had been a Soviet spy and thought of him simply as a colleague, although certainly an unusual one. We covered stories together and, on one occasion I remember, when I was stuck in Baghdad after the revolution during tight censorship, he even smuggled some of my copy out and conscientiously filed it to my newspaper from Beirut. However, despite official denials, the SIS was still strongly suspicious of his loyalty, and he was under surveillance from the moment he came to Lebanon.

When Philby arrived in Beirut, Godfrey (Paul) Paulson was MI6 station chief. He had been at Westminster School with Philby – a couple of years ahead – and was given the task of keeping an eye on him. As it transpired, Kim was certainly in touch with his Soviet control in Beirut but was too smart to be caught.

From the moment he was sacked by the SIS, however, Philby, the master spy of his generation, was effectively out of the game. Paul Paulson was authorised to give him small handouts to boost his meagre earnings, and asked him to carry out minor intelligence activities during his journalistic assignments in the Middle East. While assuming this friendly relationship, however, Paulson was playing a cat and mouse game, trying to test Kim and catch him out in any contact with the Soviet intelligence.

Just before lunch, Kim used frequently to turn up at Joe's bar, a favourite spot for MI6 and other embassy officials, almost next door to the British embassy. John Julius Norwich, then a young diplomat, remembers Philby looking a rather romantic figure in his neckerchief, always on his own, and often already almost speechless with

drink. 'I felt sorry for him,' John Julius said, 'and had always hoped
he would find a woman. But I never expected him to meet the only
person who drank as much as he did!'

During the courtship, and for a short time after Kim and Eleanor
married in 1958, Kim seemed relaxed and happy. They moved into a
pleasant top floor Beirut flat, had Kim's children out for holidays and
gave and attended lots of parties, despite the onset of Lebanon's first
civil war. However, presumably as a result of the pressure of his
double life and the inevitability of his ultimate exposure, Kim took to
drink in a big way with Eleanor running a close second. In his frequently drunken periods Kim would become insulting, abusive, make
lunges at women and not infrequently goose the hostess. But by the
next day he was usually forgiven.

A *Daily Telegraph* colleague of mine, Eric Downton, gave me an
alarming account of an evening with Kim and Eleanor when he
invited them to dinner at his apartment. They arrived very late, and
on that occasion Eleanor seemed more drunk than Kim. After an
embarrassing dinner, Eleanor flopped onto a sofa and started abus-
ing Eric's wife, coincidentally another American called Eleanor. Eric
was in the kitchen getting some drinks when Kim decided to silence
his wife, got up and quietly gave her a karate chop to the back of the
neck. She immediately went silent, her head collapsed on her chest
and, for all a horrified Eleanor Downton could tell, she might have
been dead. Eric came into the room, not having witnessed the scene,
and assumed Kim's wife had fallen asleep. Eleanor Downton frantically tried to make signals to her husband to alert him to what had
happened.

After a few more drinks, Kim apologised to Eric for his wife,
wrapped her up in a blanket and suggested the Downtons should go
to bed, and that he and his wife would leave when Eleanor awoke.
The Downtons retired uneasily but were awakened in the early hours
of the morning by the sound of a battle between the Philbys as they
hurled the Downtons' *objets d'art* at each other, including some heavy
Eskimo stone carvings. It was their last night out with the Downtons.

A more sympathetic Philby story was told to me by one of Kim's
friends and former CIA agent Miles Copeland. Kim had been at a
dinner party in Cairo given by a British Embassy couple who had also
invited Freda Utley. Freda was a formidable old English woman, a
former communist who had lived in Moscow during the purges. She
then went to the other extreme, became an American citizen and a
fanatical McCarthyite anti-communist.

Freda could be very aggressive and during the dinner apparently

gave her hostess a hard time for being too liberal in her views. The next day Kim went round to the Embassy flat with a bunch of roses and a card which read:
  'I give you Freda Utley
  To me her case is open and shutley
  I always thought Freda a bit of a bleeder,
  But perhaps I should put it more subtley.'

Confession

Kim must have had tremendous self-discipline. However drunk, he never let down his guard to give any hint of his tense double life. This made an occasion when we were out late one night in Beirut even more inexplicable. We had called into Joe's bar after a party for a final drink when Moyra, sitting next to Kim, asked him directly if he were the Third Man. He grasped her ferociously by the wrist and replied 'You know, Moyra, I always believe that loyalty to your friends is more important than anything else.' Claiming that friendship was more important than institutions or 'isms', he continued 'What would you do if you knew something awful was going to happen to a friend and only you could do something about it?'

The marks on Moyra's wrist the next morning showed, she said, how steamed up Kim must have been. But in retrospect his answer only seemed to raise more questions. Why should Kim, always so careful, virtually admit to having tipped off Maclean? And how should one interpret his EM Forsterish 'loyalty to friendship' pitch, when his life had been one of betrayal on behalf of the worst of 'isms' – the cult of Stalin?

Perhaps a more likely motive for his action was to get Maclean to defect before he could betray Philby and his co-conspirator Anthony Blunt. But Kim certainly had a strong sentimental streak – whether mawkish or genuine – an aspect of his character that made him even more repulsive to the colleagues he betrayed. An illustration of his sensitivity was given to me by Miles Copeland.

After Philby's defection Miles's wife, who had been a close friend of Eleanor Philby, received a letter from Eleanor in Moscow. She showed Miles her reply and Miles asked her to add a postscript saying that they wondered whether Kim might have been laughing up his sleeve about them all the time they had been friends in Beirut. Within a very short time they received an impassioned letter from Kim, stressing how much he valued their friendship and expressing horror that the Copelands should suspect any duplicity.

There is no question that Kim adored his father St John Philby, a rascally, outrageous old character who was probably responsible for his son's incredibly flawed and complex character. St John was one of the leading Arabian explorers and Arabists of the century. A former member of the Indian Civil Service, he became so anti-British that he was locked up for a period at the start of the Second World War on suspicion of being pro-Nazi.

He converted to Islam, became a close friend of King ibn Saud, abandoned Kim's mother Dora, took a Saudi slave girl as his second wife and became a successful businessman in Saudi Arabia. Like Kim, an outsider, he had a love–hate relationship with England, subscribed to *The Times*, was a member of the Atheneum and, whenever possible, would watch a Test Match.

In 1960, on his way back to Riyadh from London, St John stopped off in Beirut, and Kim and Eleanor brought him round for drinks at our flat. Their reunion set off a round of boozing and parties, and after a hectic night at the Kit Kat night club, Eleanor told us that she had had to undress them and put father and son to bed.

After a few days, St John had a heart attack and died in Beirut and was given a Moslem funeral. Kim seemed overwhelmed by his father's death and sank even further into drink.

At around that time, Paul Paulson was replaced as station chief by Nicholas Elliott. He was one of Kim's closest friends who had helped him get his job with *The Observer*. Despite a naive faith in Kim, which he maintained long after most of his colleagues had begun to have serious doubts, Elliott went on to be a director of the SIS.

Defection

Towards the end of the year we left Beirut for London. Only a few months later, in May 1961, I was sent back to the Lebanon by *The Sunday Telegraph* to cover the story of George Blake, another SIS agent who had just been caught spying for the KGB.

Blake had been a student at the Middle East Centre for Arabic Studies (MECAS) at Shemlan, in the mountains above Beirut, when he had been lured back to Britain and arrested. Ironically, the first person I looked up on the story after flying into Beirut was Kim.

I went round to his flat late in the morning to find it in chaos after a party with furniture overturned and bottles and glasses everywhere. Kim was looking terrible, nursing a hangover which made him even more incoherent. 'Never met Blake, never even heard of the chap till I read of his arrest,' Kim told me. This is quite likely to have been true, since the KGB would not want their agents to get together, or even know of each other's existence. Kim's appearance had strikingly deteriorated since I had last seen him. And there is little doubt that Blake's arrest and his savage 42-year prison sentence precipitated Kim's further decline before his defection.

Blake, I learned later, had been sent by the SIS to MECAS on the pretext of giving him an Arabic course prior to a Middle Eastern posting. However, the British security services had in fact learned of the presence of a highly placed traitor in their midst and Blake was one of their three top suspects. It was decided to post Blake to MECAS where he could be kept isolated and under the surveillance of two British agents pretending to be fellow students, while the case was investigated.

Once it was determined that Blake was the spy, there arose the problem of getting him back to Britain in the absence of an extradition treaty with Lebanon. Blake was therefore summoned back to London ostensibly to discuss a new high-level intelligence posting to the Middle East. He later admitted to his MI5 interrogators that he had been suspicious and had secretly visited his Soviet embassy case officer in Beirut to see if he thought it was a trap. Blake also disclosed a touch of vanity – before leaving for London he had asked to be shown the various medals he had been secretly awarded by the KGB for espionage while in their service.

After investigating the case, Blake's Soviet control told him that Moscow believed the summons to London was genuine and was likely to prove a useful move in their spy's career. It was a serious blunder for the KGB, but the case clearly alerted Kim Philby and made the task of luring him back to England, once he had been rumbled, far more difficult. The final evidence of Kim's long association with the KGB was provided by the KGB agent Anatoli Golitsyn, who defected to the CIA in Helsinki in December 1961.

After Kim's escape to the Soviet Union in January 1963, I discussed his defection with Lebanon's former security chief Emir Farid Chehab. Farid was a great friend of Britain, ever since the British sprang him from a Vichy French gaol during the Second World War, and could not understand how Philby had been allowed to escape. 'We could so easily have arranged a small accident,' he told me, clearly puzzled by the behaviour of his British colleagues.

Instead Nicholas Elliott, who by the end of 1962 had left Lebanon, was sent back, on a mission impossible, to try to persuade Kim to come home and 'face the music' – offering him some vague sort of immunity if he gave a full confession. Kim subsequently told Phillip

Knightley, the last Western journalist to interview him, that he believed he had been deliberately pushed into escaping to save the British government another security scandal and sensational trial. More probably, it was just the last in a long list of bunglings of the Philby case from which the reputation of MI6 has never really recovered. Elliott's brief, given him by the head of MI6, Sir Dick White, was to confront Kim and persuade him to return. There was a warrant for Philby's arrest, but Elliott had no instructions to use force to get Philby back to London, and not suprisingly, Kim boarded a Soviet ship in Beirut harbour a few hours after meeting Elliott.

White, the former head of MI5, had been brought in to reform MI6 and bring it to heel. He had already changed the structure of the Secret Intelligence Service and dispensed with the all-powerful regional directors, the so-called 'Robber Barons', who had been a law unto themselves. After the Philby defection fiasco, the fortunes of MI6 fell to an all-time low. Most of Philby's former friends and supporters, with the exception of Elliott who seemed to bear a charmed life, were eased out. The service became an emasculated adjunct of the Foreign Office and has remained so, thanks to a large extent to its old employee Kim Philby.

After Kim's defection I never expected we would meet again. But in fact we did have one final encounter, many years later in Moscow.

Maronites

There are many theories about the origin of Lebanon's name. The one I like best is that Arabs coming across the sunbaked Syrian desert looked up in awe at the glistening snow-capped peaks of the mountains to their West and called that country Leban – the Arab name for yoghurt.

Students at MECAS in our day, when they were not learning Arabic word lists (or keeping an eye on Philby!) used to stage a spring contest to see who could ski a hundred yards from the snowline in the hills near their centre and swim a hundred yards in the blue Mediterranean below within the shortest time. They got it down to about half an hour with elaborate planning. A competitor would ski right on to the back of a waiting truck which would career down the mountain side as he changed into a swimsuit and leapt out at the water's edge.

MECAS, called by the Lebanese 'the School for Spies', was also very much a school for scandal. The students were mainly young British diplomats and military officers, many with families, who were tightly cloistered in the Druze mountain village of Shemlan, an hour's drive from Beirut. Life in Shemlan was a combination of intensive work and occasional escape in high-spirited parties. It was a lifestyle which provided a regular diet of gossip for the expatriate community down in Beirut.

In the late 1950s I covered the evacuation of MECAS under fire, when it became the centre of a battle between Druze and Christian Lebanese forces. The school reopened, only to be driven out again during the civil war in the 1970s and it is now, sadly, disbanded.

Compared with the tensions in Jordan when we left, life in Beirut was relaxed and carefree in the first year of our stay. But once more the storm clouds were forming to threaten the brief period of peace and prosperity that Lebanon was enjoying when we arrived.

Having survived the upheavals of the Suez War, the prosperous Lebanese Christians were even more confident and arrogant about their future, seemingly oblivious to the lessons provided by their blood-stained history. With money pouring into the country from the West and Arabia, their common boast was that their country had become the Switzerland of the Middle East. Unfortunately, they possessed no gift for compromise, and could see no reason to share their wealth or political power with their Moslem and Druze countrymen. And they were unable to recognise that the new Lebanon that had been created was still no more than a tiny Christian enclave surrounded by a sea of Moslem resentment – and that as a sovereign state, Lebanon was a sham.

A major cause of modern Lebanon's bloody factional wars and political instability was the behaviour of the dominant Christian Maronites, who were contemptuous of their neighbours, and loyal only to their family and their sect. The Maronites believed that Lebanon belonged exclusively to them and in this belief, unfortunately, they were actively encouraged by the French, and later by the British and the Americans.

The Maronites, an heretical sect, founded their church in Syria in the fifth century. They only survived being engulfed by Islam by taking refuge in Mount Lebanon in the eighth century – a sanctuary they shared uneasily with another persecuted religious sect, the Druze. Once established in their mountain fastness, they did nothing to endear themselves to the surrounding Moslems by allying themselves with the Crusaders in the twelfth century – and later with the Israelis in the 1970s.

An early reference to the Maronites was made in the twelfth century by Jacques de Vitry, Bishop of Acre.

> Men armed with bows and arrows and skilful in battle, inhabit the
> mountains in considerable numbers, in the province of Phoenicia,
> not far from the town of Byblos. They are called Maronites from the
> name of a certain man, their master Maron, a heretic, who affirmed
> that there was in Jesus but one will or operation. The Christians of the
> Lebanon, dupes of this diabolical error of Maron, remained separate
> from the Church nearly five hundred years. At last their hearts being
> turned, they made a profession of the Catholic faith.

As part of the deal, the Church of Rome allowed the Maronites to
keep their liturgy in Syriac, not Latin, and for parish priests to continue
to marry.

During the Ottoman empire, the inhabitants of Mount Lebanon
were allowed a considerable degree of autonomy, so long as they
paid their taxes. But in the mid-nineteenth century, civil war broke
out in the mountains. The massacres of Maronites by the Druze
brought in French troops, and thereafter, the Ottomans were forced
to accept a *millet* or province of Mount Lebanon dominated by the
Maronite sect and protected by France.

This French connection paid even bigger dividends for France's
Christian protégés during the French mandate in the Levant after the
First World War. Out of Syria, the French carved a Greater Lebanon
incorporating Beirut, Sidon, Tyre, Tripoli and the Bekaa valley with
Mount Lebanon.

This was the legacy the French left the Maronites after they withdrew their protection in 1943 and Lebanon became independent.
The Maronites, deemed to be the largest minority in the nation,
were given the Presidency and effective political control over a nation
of Shia and Sunni Moslems, Druze and Christians – all with their own
tribal chieftains and warlords. But it was a poisoned gift since in
Greater Lebanon the Maronites were far outnumbered by the other
sects, whose birth rates rapidly outstripped that of the Christians.

In 1957, 14 years after independence, none of these problems
appeared to concern the Christians or temper their optimism about
the future of Lebanon. But they were already on the road to a civil
war which proved far more bloody than under the Ottomans, and
which led to the near destruction of Beirut, the last of the great cities
of the Levant.

By the time Moyra and I arrived, Britain and the United States had
taken over the role of the French, backing the militantly Maronite
government of President Camille Chamoun, allying Lebanon to the
West and steering it towards disaster.

Getting Through

'Is there much more of this, then?' was a familiar response of the bored newspaper copy-taker to a far-flung correspondent, desperately trying to dictate his story on an awful phone line. Communications, visas and censorship were the three biggest problems in covering the Middle East or other parts of the Third World. Writing the story was the easy bit.

Copy-takers were often men with a short interest span, working late at night and wishing they were home, operating with two fingers on ancient typewriters in need of care and attention. 'Hang on a moment, this needs a new ribbon' or 'oops the key's fallen off' were the sort of remarks that greeted you after frustrating hours spent while waiting for your phone call to London. 'Can't hear a word you're saying, you'd better phone in again', followed by a click as he puts the receiver down – and you knew you would probably never get through again that night, and that your day's work had been in vain.

A cardinal rule for a foreign correspondent was – be very, very nice to copy-takers. One colleague of mine during the Falklands War finally got a call through to London from Buenos Aires. He began to dictate a story about Argentinian press attacks against Britain which so incensed the copy-taker that he exclaimed 'I'm not having any more of this anti-British propaganda' and cut him off.

During the frequent periods of coups, assassinations or civil wars in the Middle East, however, the authorities normally cut off the phones and cables in any case. The only solution then was to fly the copy out yourself, and risk not being able to return to cover the rest of the story, or persuade someone to take it over for you. As a result, I have spent many desperate hours in airports all over the world trying to persuade air travellers – businessmen, rival journalists, airline crew – to slip an uncensored press cable into their pocket. Despite the dangers involved, it was surprising how many agreed. Now, however, with TV crews travelling with their own communications systems and satellite-linked telephones, it is almost impossible for a state to impose effective censorship except by threatening correspondents with expulsion if their reports displease.

The Jordan story and the struggle for survival of the young King continued to be my main news focus, and a running battle with censorship, in my first year with the *Chronicle*.

In the spring of 1957, while covering Ali Abu Nuwar's unsuccessful coup against King Hussein, a frustrated world press, which had flocked into Amman to witness what was widely expected to be the death throes of the Hashemite monarchy, found itself under 24-hour curfew and unable to file the story. Outside the small hotel – the Amman Club – inside which we were all confined, grim-looking Bedouin troops with blackened faces and armed with rifles and pick handles patrolled the empty streets.

Inside, correspondents who included Joe Alsop of the *New York Herald Tribune*, Sam Brewer, Kim Philby, and others found themselves with nothing to do but drink and write stories and features which they had no way of filing. In the lounge a Sicilian band, trapped with us, played and replayed its very limited repertoire throughout the day. In desperation we took up a collection for the band to buy their silence. But this only angered them and they played even louder.

After three long days, when we had all written ourselves to a stand-still, the curfew was lifted for two hours. Clutching sheaves of copy we raced to the cable office. There we were told that everything had to be passed by the censor who was to be found at the government radio station just out of town.

About 50 of us arrived in taxis at the radio station gates. The censor was unwell and would not see us, we were told by the guards. We began a noisy demonstration of our own until the censor relented and allowed two of the press to bring up the huge stack of copy. They found him on the second floor, magnificently drunk, lying on an army camp bed with a bottle of scotch beside him. With curfew time running out, we waited in the wasteland outside the radio sta-tion until eventually a piece of paper fluttered down from the censor's window and landed on a camel thorn bush. It was, I seem to remember, take four of a long feature for *The Wall Street Journal*.

Other bits of paper then began to descend, some covered in blue pencil, others pristine - just as the light began to fade. When we finally dashed for the cable office most of us clutched at least one piece of paper – perhaps just a disjointed insert or an add to a story that still lay beside the censor's camp bed, or might even then be drifting down through the desert night.

Waugh-Land

'ADEN UNWARWISE'. That was how Corker, the Fleet Street newsagency man, in cables described the situation in the British colony in Evelyn Waugh's *Scoop*.

Aden was still 'unwarwise', and cables still in use, some 20 years later when I first arrived there to cover the sort of story Waugh would have savoured. By chance, my visit coincided with the start of a pattern of events that was to lead remorselessly, within a decade, to Britain's surrender to terrorism and anarchy, and its abandonment of Aden and the Protectorate to the Soviet bloc.

Aden was then one of the world's busiest harbours and in the port hundreds of little Indian and Arab shops did a brisk trade in duty-free radios, cameras and watches. There had been a brief blip in the Colony's prosperity when Nasser blocked the Suez canal, but the canal had now reopened and it was business as usual.

Britain, thrown out of Egypt and Jordan and with Cyprus in revolt was looking for a new Middle East base to protect the Gulf and the oilfields, and to act as a staging post East of Suez to the Far East. Aden was the choice, the 'arsehole of the Empire' as the garrison called it. It was established by Britain as a coaling station in 1839 – the first ter-ritory to be acquired in the reign of Queen Victoria – and still looked it. It became a Crown Colony in 1935 and in the 1960s was joined to a British-sponsored Federation of South Arabia which collapsed a few years later.

By the time I arrived there on my first visit the government of Harold Macmillan, seeking to restore Britain's strategic position in the East after its defeat in Egypt, had decided to convert Aden into a major strategic military base. A huge BP oil refinery had already been built and a new airbase was under construction.

What was also new was the rash of pictures of Gamal Abdel Nasser grinning toothily from almost every shop in the bazaar, and the daily attacks on British imperialism broadcast by 'The Voice of the Arabs'. The local population was clearly thrilled by the defeat of Britain, France and Israel in the Suez War, but in this remote part of South Arabia there was no indication that the British authorities were taking seriously the lesson of Suez and the intoxicating effects of Arab nationalism.

I came, in 1957, to cover Aden's first general strike and had been invited to stay with friends – the young American Consul General Bill Crawford and his wife Ginger. I had only planned to spend a few days but became 'the man who came to dinner' as the news story developed.

Bill was also US representative to the neighbouring, medieval Kingdom of Yemen. From time to time he would load up his jeep with suitcases of silver Maria Theresa thalers, the only acceptable currency in Yemen, and set out for Sanaa to try for an audience with Yemen's despotic old ruler.

Imam Ahmad — the king and head of Yemen's dominant Zaidi Moslems – was a hard man to meet. A gross, fearsome-looking chieftain with mad, popping eyes and a dyed-black beard, the Imam had survived frequent assassination attempts and terrorised his kingdom. He suffered from a plethora of diseases and these, combined with his age and corpulence, increased his obsession about his sexual performance. As an aid to sexual intercourse he employed Italian engineers at his palace to build a powered rocking bed, found in the ruins of his palace after a later anti-royalist coup, designed to reduce his physical exertions while on the job. On one occasion, after a course of hormone drugs supplied by American doctors, he summoned his household to observe and celebrate his achievement of an erection.

After many attempts at a meeting, Bill Crawford told me he was suddenly summoned from the government guest-house late one night for an audience. He was confronted by this startling figure, seated on a raised dais, who wanted a discussion on world politics. Much of what he said made sense, said Bill, but during the conversation the Imam 'seemed to fade in and out like an old radio set'.

The Imam, who was certainly odd but by no means gaga, had recently established relations with Moscow and Peking, and a Soviet freighter filled with arms and ammunition had just arrived in Yemen. Some of these were quickly distributed to tribes in the Aden Protectorate and a few days after my arrival in Aden, the British had a full-scale uprising on their hands.

Until then tribal troubles had been easily put down, but the one in the Emirate of Dhala set a new pattern. In the years that followed larger and larger British forces were drawn into the fighting in the Protectorate. This, combined with increasing terrorism, bombings and assassinations in Aden, led to Britain's final withdrawal and the British presence was replaced by a bunch of thugs from East Germany, Cuba and Czechoslovakia.

The Dhala story had everything for the British press - a young British political agent with the romantic name of FitzRoy Somerset besieged, with a small garrison of Arab levies, in a remote mountain fort by tribesmen in the pay of the Imam. We flew with the RAF in strafing raids against the tribesmen surrounding the fort and finally went in with the troops who broke the siege.

As the story developed, the press poured into Aden's Crescent Hotel – a gloomy relic of the Raj where the British community drank their pink gins in semi-darkness away from the glare of the Arabian sun. For the next ten years, the lugubrious Crescent was to become one of the centres for the international press covering Middle Eastern crises, along with the St. Georges in Beirut and the Ledra

Palace in Nicosia. Of the three the 'Ledra P.', as it was known, was probably the best organised to meet the peculiar needs of that rumbustious, endlessly demanding, restless and competitive tribe – the foreign press. This was due largely to a hotel employee who displayed an instant perception of the mysterious workings of the press and how to exploit it.

He was able to rely on a steady stream of correspondents to cover *EOKA* terrorist attacks against the British, intercommunal violence between Greek and Turk and finally the long-awaited Turkish invasion of Cyprus. For a modest fee on arrival he would take good care of you. He would read the cables of your rivals to ensure you were never scooped, and send out his spies to scour the bars and restaurants for you whenever a story broke in your absence to ensure that you would not miss your edition. At the end of your stay, if requested, he would produce an imaginative second hotel bill especially tailored to your needs, along with receipts to be used as evidence for expenses claims.

This service sometimes even stretched to advance information about terrorist attacks enabling a reporter to get to the spot, usually on Ledra Street's 'Murder Mile' just as the shot was being fired or the bomb exploded. There were times, however, when his efforts to please did overstep the mark. One colleague passing the reception desk noticed the employee's writing on the press cable he had handed in earlier to be sent to the cable office. Asked what he was doing, the employee explained that he had decided the story was not strong enough and was changing the lead.

In Aden, the most visible member of the press to take up residence at the Crescent Hotel to cover the Dhala story was the *Evening Standard* correspondent Randolph Churchill – an old comrade in arms of Evelyn Waugh who could well have invented him. He was both an outrageous and a tragic figure, roving the world as a newspaper correspondent, mostly drunk, alienated from his father, with two failed marriages behind him. He could be amusing, witty, generous and incredibly rude. With Randolph, it was like being next to a bomb that you knew was going to explode. His usual apology on the morning after was 'I should never be allowed out in private'.

On arrival in Aden, he asked me up to his room where he had summoned a masseuse as well as a secretary, since he had never learned to type. With a bottle of scotch to hand, he lay on a table like a beached whale as the masseuse worked on him while he dictated his despatch. Randolph was only in his late forties, but already looked ancient. Observing his shambling figure on the beach one day, one of his colleagues said to me 'he's the only man I've ever seen who looks older than his father'.

Randolph was on an anti-American kick throughout his stay, convinced that the US was backing Yemen in stirring up trouble in the Aden Protectorate. At one point, he became so insulting about America in the Crescent bar that a normally mild American correspondent threw his drink in Randolph's face. To everyone's surprise Randolph just turned round and walked away.

By the time the press was flown into the base of the mountain to watch British and Aden troops storm the besieged fort, I was about the only colleague still on good terms with Randolph, who had been cheerfully exploiting the family name to get special treatment from the military and the RAF in covering the story. Most of us had just brought a sandwich or two along, so when Randolph worked a lift in an RAF plane back to Aden to file an early story for the *Standard*, he kindly bequeathed his lunch to me. It contained roast chickens, pies, eggs and bottles of wine which provided a picnic in the desert for about eight of us.

It was like covering a colonial war from the nineteenth century except for the air strikes against the surrounding tribesmen. A company of the Buffs and a company of Aden levies, under sniper fire, finally stormed a 2,000 foot escarpment and relieved the fort from its eight-day siege. During the next few years, tribal uprisings in the Protectorate, backed by Yemen and Egypt, escalated and drew in thousands of British troops. The SAS played an increasingly prominent role. In 1964, when one of its operations went badly, an SAS captain and a trooper were killed and their heads exhibited on stakes in the Yemeni town of Tiaz.

At the end of the Dhala affair, I flew back to Beirut and started telling Moyra about my exploits in Southern Arabia. As I was talking, I noticed there was no glass in the windows of our apartment. 'You never gave me a chance to tell you,' she said. 'There was a bomb outside the building last night when we were asleep and we were covered in glass.' Neither she nor our daughters, Jennifer and Fiona were hurt, but the first Lebanese civil war – a dress rehearsal for the big one – had begun.

Lebanon Warwise

Within days, in the midst of an economic boom, Lebanon was plunged into chaos and anarchy. It was a tragedy waiting to happen.

The Lebanese Christians were becoming increasingly rich and self-satisfied, while the Moslems, with little share in the growing prosperity, were being constantly stirred up by the growing force of Arab nationalism.

In Beirut, barricades were thrown up all over the city between Christian and Moslem sectors. Tripoli, Tyre and Sidon fell into the hands of rebel forces, heavy fighting erupted in the mountains between the Maronites and the Druze and the Bekaa valley between Lebanon and Syria became a no man's land.

The CIA and MI6 helped set the stage for the confrontation by purchasing a landslide victory for the supporters of the pro-Western President Camille Chamoun – the handsome, conniving Maronite and former Lebanese ambassador to Britain. Bill Eveland, one of the CIA agents there, subsequently described how he travelled regularly to the presidential palace with his briefcase stuffed with Lebanese pounds, returning late at night to the American embassy to replenish the slush fund.

Chamoun was seen by America and Britain as a bulwark against communism and the ambitions of President Nasser, and he was actively encouraged and financed, in breach of the Lebanese constitution, to stand for a second term of office. It seemed to London and Washington like a good idea at the time, but it led to disaster.

After the Suez fiasco, Beirut became the regional headquarters of SIS operations in the Middle East, while Britain's loss of power and influence opened the way for a surge of Soviet agents and military advisers into the Arab world.

SIS officers working for Paul Paulson in Beirut under diplomatic cover outnumbered the real diplomats there. Remarkably, none of them were Arabists and were forced to rely heavily on Embassy contacts, especially those of Maroun Arab, the Embassy's Lebanese-born Oriental Counsellor whose sources were largely limited to Lebanese Christians. A youngish Palestinian employed in a key role in running anti-Nasser propaganda was later found to be a double agent, working for Egyptian intelligence on the side.

One of the British intelligence officers, perhaps taking a leaf out of Graham Greene's book *Our Man In Havana*, recruited a Lebanese to run a bogus spy ring. Tens of thousands of pounds of SIS funds were provided to meet the salaries and expenses of these fictitious agents. The fraud was finally exposed after London control noticed that intelligence reports from their costly Levant spy ring regularly increased whenever the budget for the operation came up for review. 'Our Man In Beirut' was finally sacked.

MI6 ran its operation from its own top security floor in the drab British embassy building on rue de Phoenicia, known to all Beirut as the 'Spears Mission' the unofficial branch office of which was Joe's bar. General Spears had been appointed by Winston Churchill during the Second World War to head the British military mission to Syria and Lebanon. Allied troops drove out the pro-Nazi Vichy French forces and Spears, once a well-known Francophile, kicked out the French administration and became a local hero.

Earlier in the war, the Vichy French, under pressure from the Germans, had banished the last two remaining members of the British Consulate in Beirut to the Lebanese mountain resort of Aley. One of the diplomats – Philip Adams – a friend of ours who came back to Beirut as British regional information officer in 1956, told me what happened next.

With little to do in Aley, Philip and his colleague, Geoffrey Furlonge, took up plane spotting and, with the aid of a wartime air-craft manual, identified a fleet of *Luftwaffe* aircraft flying across the Lebanese mountains to refuel at the French Air Force Rayak airbase in the Bekaa valley. The planes were on their way to Baghdad, flying in supplies to support a pro-Axis revolt by a group of Iraqi generals which could have had a devastating strategic affect on the course of the war. Adams and Furlonge managed to signal the RAF in Palestine, which promptly attacked Rayak and destroyed most of the German aircraft on the ground. One plane that did get through to Baghdad, carrying a senior German general, was shot down by mistake by the mutineers, and shortly afterwards the revolt collapsed.

There were, however, no such dramatic intelligence coups by the British in Lebanon in the late 1950s against the spreading influence of President Nasser and his Soviet ally. Heavy-handed interference in the Lebanese elections only made things worse for the Western cause.

Moderate Lebanese politicians, who found themselves out in the cold as a result of the rigged elections, were outraged, while pro-Nasser fervour was fired up by the union, early in 1958, of Egypt and Syria. Money and arms poured in from Damascus for the rebels and in the face of mounting atrocities and terrorism, the Lebanese Army, half Christian, half Moslem, and commanded by the Maronite General Fuad Shehab, only managed to hold together by staying more or less neutral.

Covering for the *News Chronicle* what the Lebanese called euphemistically 'les événements' entailed much nervous clambering through barricades during lulls in the fighting to interview the various tribal leaders, and travelling uneasily across the country without ever knowing quite who was shooting at whom. A group of us having been fired at on our way to Tripoli, found the culprit – a very small Lebanese boy clutching a rifle he was barely able to hold. He said his father had left him there to go for lunch and told him to shoot anybody he saw coming up the road.

One of the oddest excursions I made was to Mukhtara the castle of the Druze feudal leader and eccentric, Kamal Jumblatt. A curious feature of the place, high up in the Shouf mountains, was a fast-flowing stream running past the reception room right through the middle of the castle. Jumblatt, a mild-looking rebel leader in a lounge suit, was surrounded by fierce Druze warriors brandishing guns, knives and bandoliers. He claimed he was really a pacifist and follower of Gandhi – a philosophy which did not seem to deter his gunmen from committing some of the worst atrocities of the war.

Despite the bombings, sniping and curfews, it was pretty well business as usual for Beirut's nightlife. In the midst of it all my mother came out from London for a holiday, determined to enjoy herself. Fortunately all the nightclubs kept open – you just had to stay in them until dawn when the curfew was lifted, and this seemed to suit her very well!

Communications, as ever, were tricky. With no long-distance telephone calls or telex available, the only way to file a story was to take the press cable to the main post office. It was located in the centre of town next to the Moslem quarter – a bad area for sniping and cross-fire.

When I was working on a late story, Moyra used to leave our two daughters with our Lebanese maid in order to file my early copy on the fighting. After driving through town she would wait for a lull in the firing, sprint across the square to the cable office and then search out the military censor who had to look at the story before it could be sent. The censor would then routinely delete all references to Christians and Moslems, causing much confusion when the story, usually recounting the day's sectarian clashes, landed on the desk.

I suppose we were both lucky not to get shot. John Julius Norwich was less fortunate. He used to drive a noisy three-wheel bubble car and heard a loud bang when passing an army check-point on his way home. It was not until he arrived back in his house that he was aware of blood on his face from a bullet that had grazed his head.

In the middle of the war, we moved into a flat next to John Julius after it had been unexpectedly vacated by Lieutenant Colonel Alec Brodie, the Embassy military attaché. It was right on no man's land between the Christian and Moslem Basta quarter overlooking the barricaded house of Saeb Salaam, the opposition Sunni Moslem leader. The flat had a huge veranda with a magnificent view of the city and harbour – a ringside seat of the war, illuminated at night by tracers and gunfire. Its only disadvantage was the mosque right opposite which used to blast out on a loudspeaker the call for dawn prayers through the night, and on Fridays delivered a long sermon, usually denouncing British imperialism.

The flat became vacant after Moslem gunmen had burst into it and seized Alec's Lebanese servant whom they suspected of firing on them from the balcony. Alec managed to save him from summary execution but had to move out of the apartment.

Alec, an officer of the Black Watch, was reputed to be the most highly wounded serving member of the British Army and a legend to his regiment. Astonished Lebanese soldiers would see him in his kilt and full regalia, charging all over the country wherever there was a battle. On one occasion in the Bekaa valley, he was busily advising a Lebanese Army NCO where to set up a machine-gun post, when he was tapped on the shoulder by General Shehab who had to remind him politely who was in charge!

Amidst all this chaos of civil war, English eccentrics stayed on. One of our near neighbours who remained throughout the fighting was an elderly English spinster devoted to her large family of cats. She used to feed them in the courtyard below our apartment, and I once overheard her admonishing them 'I don't want to catch you talking to those Moslem cats'.

Death of a King

The events of 1958 unfortunately provided no lessons for the far greater horrors of the Lebanese Civil War of the late 1970s and 1980s. A generation later, Lebanon once again saw the breakdown of the political system, and the country returned to tribalism, terrorist bombings, atrocities and anarchy.

But on 14 July 1958 an event occurred which once more was to transform the situation in the Middle East, bringing about American military intervention in the Lebanon and breaking the cycle of violence there. The bloody overthrow of the Iraqi monarchy on that day caught the West completely by surprise and within two days the US marines were in Beirut and a British paratroop brigade was landing in Amman.

The day after the Iraqi coup we were having lunch in our flat, which overlooked the Mediterranean, with John Mossman, an old friend and colleague who had been sent to Beirut by the *Daily Herald*. Gradually we saw a growing number of dots on the horizon approaching the coast. Running through a beach crowded with sunbathers, we were just in time to watch as amphibious tanks eerily surfaced through the waves and stood on the shore rotating their gun turrets. They were followed by fearsome-looking marines from the US Sixth Fleet who leapt into the surf from landing craft. They were loaded with machine-guns, mortars and flame-throwers, and muttered 'excuse me Ma'am' as they advanced past sunbathers in bikinis, while Lebanese beach boys tried to sell them Cokes and ice creams.

President Dwight. D. Eisenhower had decided to send in 15,000 US Marines, officially in response to an appeal from President Chamoun who claimed his country was under threat from Egypt and Syria. However, Eisenhower's decision had been triggered by the Iraqi Revolution. This had instantly sparked Western fears of the total collapse of its position in the Arab World and a takeover by Pro-Nasser forces, widely believed to be hand in glove with Moscow.

The American landing was unopposed, but unfortunately Chamoun had neglected to inform his Army Commander General Shehab of his call for US intervention. As the Marines left the beach and headed for Beirut airport they were halted by a Lebanese Army column, and a tense standoff ensued until a message arrived from Chamoun confirming that the Americans had been invited in.

All Beirut hospitals had been placed on full alert, but they didn't actually have a casualty until my two-year-old daughter Fiona fell down and cut her nose rather badly. Moyra drove her in the MG to the American hospital in Beirut where she found empty emergency wards and five surgeons waiting to attend to her.

The Iraqi Revolution was a dramatic new defeat for Anglo-American policy. It was a special blow to Britain, which monopolised Iraq's oil and in effect ran the country through its ambassador Sir Michael Wright in league with Iraq's veteran politician and Prime Minister Nuri Said.

Three years earlier, Britain had stitched together the Baghdad Pact, an ill-conceived anti-Soviet alliance involving Iraq, Iran and Turkey. Two days before the Iraqi Revolution, the Pact held a strategy meeting in Istanbul attended by Wright and a junior British diplomat Anthony Parsons, who had been an assistant military attaché in Baghdad. During the meeting Parsons asked Wright when he expected a 'Nasser-style' revolution in Iraq. He received an angry response from Wright, who told him stiffly that Nuri Said had everything under control.

Ironically, 20 years later, Sir Anthony Parsons, then ambassador to Iran found himself in a very similar position to Wright and, in turn, seriously underestimated the anti-Western forces that overthrew the Shah. Parsons later admitted that he, like Wright in his day, had been out of touch and had not recognised the warnings that robbed Britain of an ally and one of its best customers.

The Iraqi Revolution came about, indirectly, as the result of a plot by the CIA, backed by Britain, to destabilise the pro-Nasser regime in Syria which was threatening neighbouring Lebanon and Jordan. As part of these moves, Nuri Said had agreed to send a brigade of Iraqi troops to take up positions near the Jordan–Syrian border and intervene in the event of a revolt in Syria.

They were commanded by a highly unstable Iraqi Brigadier Abdel Karim Kassem. Normally Iraqi Army units were deprived of live ammunition in case they should attempt a coup. However, Kassem's brigade was permitted to pass by Baghdad fully armed on its way to the Jordan frontier, but instead it turned its guns on the royal palace.

Young King Feisal, his uncle Crown Prince Abdul Illah and the male and female members of the royal family were lined up against the palace wall and shot. Nuri Said escaped from his home disguised as a woman but was spotted and torn to pieces by the Baghdad mob. The British Embassy was sacked and Sir Michael Wright and his staff narrowly escaped the fate of the prime minister.

Desert Journey

As soon as I had covered the marine landings, I dashed to Amman just in time to witness the arrival from Cyprus of the first plane-load of British paras. The idea was to back King Hussein and prevent an anti-monarchist Iraqi-style revolution in Jordan.

The paras set up a few tents in the middle of the airfield, but looked a small and vulnerable bunch of men as we waited in vain for the armada of planes flying in the rest of the Brigade. It turned out that Britain had neglected to obtain permission to overfly Israel and after the first plane arrived Israel closed its airspace. The paras therefore spent a lonely night while negotiations with the Israelis were under way, until finally the rest of the Brigade flew in escorted by US Navy warplanes.

The world press meanwhile had been pouring into Beirut for the competition to be first into Baghdad. All Iraqi frontier posts and airports had been closed amid reports of horrifying mob scenes and violence. Most of the press set up temporary bureaux at the St Georges

Hotel and were concentrating on trying to charter planes and pilots
who would be prepared to risk their lives flying in.

John Mossman and I went to Damascus and hailed a taxi off the
street and asked the driver to take us to Baghdad. We loaded up with
some Arabic bread, bottles of beer, a compass, a school atlas from a
local bookshop and a lot of petrol. The driver claimed he knew the
way, but we knew it was no use taking the regular route through
Jordan where we would be stopped at the frontier and sent back.
Instead, we made a wide 700-mile swing, very hot and dusty, through
the Syrian desert, guided by our atlas and the occasional vehicle
tracks.

Just as we were setting out from Damascus, an enthusiastic young
Egyptian newspaper photographer from the *Al Ahram* newspaper
rushed up and asked if he could come along. He certainly saved our
expedition and may have saved our lives.

After a 30-hour journey, we crossed the desert into Iraq. We
then started running into road blocks manned by villainous-looking
Iraqi soldiers, some of whom showed us with delight photos of dis-
membered bodies of the old regime. The favourite pastime of the
Baghdad mob had been to drag the dead or dying tied behind cars
and trucks through the streets of the city.

Everyone was wildly pro-Nasser and each time we hit a road block
our photographer would leap out, announce he was Egyptian, point
his empty camera at the troops, take their names and tell them that
his paper would send them the pictures. It worked every time and we
were allowed through.

During the journey John was sitting in the back with the photographer and I was in front with the driver. From time to time John
complained to me that the photographer was getting rather
amorous. I declined his suggestion to change places but pointed out
that he would have to put up with it if we were going to reach
Baghdad. He was much relieved when we finally arrived at the
Baghdad Hotel where Sir Michael Wright had taken refuge after his
embassy had been sacked and partly burned.

The hotel was still in a state of shock after the atrocities of a few
days before, of which we were given chilling accounts. On the day of
the revolution troops arrived and rounded up all Western guests and
a delegation of Jordanian politicians and Army officers. They were
lined up in the foyer and then loaded on to buses to be taken off to
detention. Two resourceful British businessmen climbed into the
bus and then quietly got out the other side and stood unobserved
with a crowd of hotel staff. The rest were driven off by the Army but

the convoy was attacked by the mob. Several of the hotel guests were torn to pieces, including two Jordanian government ministers.

The deputy chief of staff of the Jordanian Army told me how he managed to fight his way through the crowd, badly mauled, and reached the yard of the defence ministry. He was left lying there all day until he was finally taken to a hospital ward where Iraqi officers would come each day to spit on him and insult him.

When John and I finally reached our hotel rooms, we worked out an escape route from our bedrooms through the gardens and a swim across the Tigris in case of another round-up. It had been a long day but I waited for John to get to sleep before I thundered on his door and shouted in Arabic for him to come out. I don't think he ever forgave me.

We were delighted that our two papers, with the most modest financial resources in Fleet Street, had been the first to reach Baghdad despite the wealthy competition. But having announced our arrival, there was not much we could file because of the censorship which permitted only nice things to be said about the Iraqis and their new leaders. The next battle was obtaining an exit visa to get out to tell the real story.

The British Embassy had had a particularly rough time. Its staff, including the Ambassador and his wife, had been trapped in a secure part of the chancery while a mob looted and set fire to the building. Finally some Iraqi troops broke through and told the British to come out. It looked like a choice between being burned to death or torn to pieces, but, improbably, the soldiers managed to save them.

One of my favourite stories concerned Lady Wright, an imperious figure, a sort of Marie Antoinette of the Iraqi Revolution. On the morning before the revolution Lady Wright was being driven across the desert to Baghdad in the Embassy Rolls from the RAF station at Habbaniya. Her driver was a British army sergeant who was reaching the end of his tether with her Ladyship. Suddenly, halfway across the desert, the car stopped and the sergeant began to get out. 'What's the matter, what's the matter?' cried Lady Wright, rapping impatiently on the dividing window. 'The car appears to have broken down, your Ladyship' replied the sergeant. 'But Rolls Royces never break down', she exclaimed. 'Well this bugger has,' said her driver, who was saved just in time from disciplinary action by the revolution.

But Lady Wright, by all accounts, like the Queen of France behaved with great bravery and dignity when facing the mob. Later, I spoke to her in her hotel suite and asked her about her experience and how she now felt about Iraq. 'Oh I still love my Iraqis,' she replied with a gracious smile.

A year later, I returned to Baghdad for the celebrations of the first 12 months of republican Iraq – and what a difference a year had made! After 12 bloodstained months of crisis and strife in the Middle East, the unpredictable leader of the Iraqi coup, President Abdel Karim Kassem, had fought back the pro-Nasser nationalist forces in Iraq and was now turning on the powerful communist party.

Events had moved swiftly since the previous July. Then, I had arrived to find the British residency in smoking ruins with mobs gloating over the murder of their young king and his uncle. Everyone was hailing Nasser as the hero of the revolution. His photograph was everywhere – but a year later anyone trying to display it would be torn to pieces.

Immediately after the coup, the citizens of Baghdad were obediently cursing the name of Abdel Nasser and praising 'our sole leader' – a title which could sound unfortunate when pronounced quickly in English – as the nation's saviour. Kassem had achieved his coup more by luck than judgement. Sitting through endless hours of a rambling interview I had with him in the ministry of defence he made no sense at all and was probably certifiably mad. But he was also cunning. Both Nasser and the communists had made the mistake of underestimating him and were paying the price.

After the first, shocked reaction to the brutalities of the Iraqi Revolution, Britain had adopted a realistic policy towards the new republic, and it was paying off. The British government went out on a much-criticised limb by selling arms to Kassem at a critical stage in his relations with the Soviet bloc, thereby enabling him to avoid total dependence on communist sources. Meanwhile, he had been building up within his army a bloc of Iraqi nationalists without ties to either the communists or pro-Nasser elements and was eliminating the communist-dominated Popular Resistance Forces which sprang up during the Revolution.

Perhaps one of the most astonishing turnarounds over the past year was Kassem's relations with the extremely shrewd new British ambassador, Sir Humphrey Trevelyan. When Sir Humphrey arrived Britain – the power that had dominated Iraq for over 40 years – was top of the list of the new republic's suspects. Trevelyan, however, (described by his friends as a big-eared Cornish gnome!) was the complete opposite of the usual British Proconsul. He had tremendous powers of charm and persuasion and within months it was to him that Kassem, beset by problems posed by both communists and Arab nationalists, frequently came for advice.

Sir Humphrey was also superb when dealing with the press, a quality rarely found in senior British diplomats. He would normally invite you to his study in the evening after work. Over a bottle of scotch, he would provide you with a very frank and fascinating insight into what was going on in the country – and you would usually leave totally persuaded by his point of view!

Kassem, after his first year in office, still had very large quantities of cash to squander – the legacy of a careful and, by Middle East standards, well-regulated development fund consisting of Iraq's oil royalties and overseen by British advisers.

The anniversary day began with a huge military parade of Soviet tanks, artillery and aircraft that had flowed into Iraq over the past year. Both Russia and China had sent over their deputy foreign ministers. The next three days saw a programme for diplomats and press of gruelling tours of industrial projects – dams and factories and power stations intended to advertise the achievements of the new republic. Every one of them were projects by the Kingdom of Iraq's development board and had been at the point of completion at the time of the revolution.

Four years later, I was back in Baghdad for *The Daily Telegraph* to cover President Kassem's assassination – a new stage in Iraq's decline into a pariah state.

The remainder of my time with the *News Chronicle* before I was sent to cover the upheavals in the Belgian Congo was mainly concerned with the stormy events in the Arab world and the continued unrest in Cyprus. But in the spring of 1960, serious trouble was brewing in Turkey and I flew to Ankara with the BBC correspondent Erik de Mauny.

Growing discontent over an economic crisis and a crackdown on the opposition had brought thousands of students out on the streets to demonstrate against Premier Adnan Menderes and his government. The demonstrations had been joined by army cadets whom the Army, brought in to restore law and order, were reluctant to attack.

For Menderes it was a sudden reversal of fortune. Only months before he had had a miraculous escape from death when he emerged almost unscathed after his airliner had crashed in Britain. All Ankara had turned out to welcome his return. A British diplomat who witnessed the scene reported seeing cars skidding out of control on the blood of hundreds of camels sacrificed at the roadside to celebrate Menderes' escape.

However, since the economic slump, the situation was running out of control. There had been riots in parliament and one young British embassy official, just posted to Ankara and making his first visit to the foreign ministry, witnessed Turkish cavalry with sabres drawn charging large crowds of demonstrators.

On the day we arrived, Erik and I contacted the opposition Republican Party spokesman, Bulent Ecevit, a very bright young politician who later became prime minister. He insisted on taking us for a very late night out and prophesied a big story for the next day. We returned to our hotel at about two in the morning and a few hours later I was awoken by the sound of gunfire. My bedroom windows looked onto a main square and as I drew the curtains I had a ringside view of the coup. A column of army cadets from the military academy was marching in to surround the city, infantry and cavalry were mustered on the hill where the British embassy stands while *Patton* tanks moved across the square.

"It's a coup, Erik!' I shouted, as I dashed into his bedroom where he was still fast asleep. We rushed up to the hotel roof to get a better view, but by now bullets were flying and we decided to retreat.

Within hours, Menderes, Turkey's President Celal Bayar, foreign minister Orlu (known as 'Mr Seven Percent' for the profit he exacted on government deals) and most of the cabinet had been picked up. The recently resigned commander of Turkish ground forces, white-haired General Cemal Gursel (known as 'uncle' to his troops) headed the coup.

By Middle East standards it was a relatively bloodless operation, but turned out to be considerably more vindictive than most of us expected. Western diplomats at first assumed that the army would be a moderating influence on the Turkish political scene. But within days 400 members of parliament and five generals had been arrested and sent to the prison island of Yassiada on the Sea of Marmora.

In an eerie scene I attended the day after the coup, the new military regime trooped over to the mausoleum where the body of Kemal Ataturk, founder of modern Turkey lay. Ataturk had become a cult in Turkey – almost a god. With piped military music in the background, General Gursel stepped forward and spoke to Ataturk's body, asking his blessing on the actions the military had taken.

After a long trial and a lot of trumped-up charges, Menderes, a world-class statesman, Zorlu and other ministers and supporters were sentenced to hang. The sentence sent a shockwave through the Western world and American, French and British leaders all pleaded with the Turkish government to spare Menderes' life, to no avail. After Menderes had been hanged, the British Ambassador to Turkey, Sir Bernard Borroughs, was heard to comment that, knowing the stubbornness of the Turks, Western appeals would have only made them more determined to hang Menderes. 'If we'd kept our mouths shut' said Borroughs 'he might have stood a chance.'

4

Congo

The horrors of the Iraqi Revolution were small-scale compared with the events which erupted in the Congo when the Belgians lost their nerve and cut and ran. By that time, things had begun to calm down in the Middle East, apart from the occasional coup or political assassination. I was beginning to enjoy the sort of life that all foreign editors suspect to be the normal lifestyle of their correspondents abroad – a day on the ski slopes or lying on the beach with a transistor radio protectively tuned into the BBC World Service.

Stories of raped nuns, Belgian refugees pouring out of the Congo and tribal massacres began to fill the headlines in the wake of Congolese independence. 'We are no longer your monkies,' Premier Patrice Lumumba told King Baudouin during the independence ceremony on 30 June 1960. It was all downhill after that.

The country was totally unprepared for independence with no blacks in the army above the rank of sergeant and practically no university graduates or senior civil servants.

Within days, the *Force Publique*, entirely officered by Belgians, had mutinied, and a stream of frightened Belgian officers and civil servants and businessmen, often preceding their families, fled across the Congo into Brazzaville or over the borders into Southern Rhodesia. The United Nations flew in troops to try to restore order, and the Congo's richest province, Katanga, backed by the *Union Minière*, Belgian troops and mercenaries, declared independence.

The vast Belgian Congo had come into being when King Leopold II of the Belgians carved it out of the heart of Africa and ran it as his private estate. Belgium's atrocious treatment of the African population was exposed by the Irish revolutionary Sir Roger Casement when he was in the British Consular Service.

When I arrived in Leopoldville, later to become Kinshasa, in

September 1960 for the *News Chronicle*, the Congo, in a state of chaos and anarchy, had become a focal point of the Cold War, a battle-ground for the heart of Africa.

The Congolese Prime Minister, a wild, erratic former postal clerk, had become a hero of the communist bloc and the Third World. But he had signed his own death warrant by appealing for Soviet arms and Czech technicians to bolster his army. In response, the Soviet bloc had overplayed its hand, and flown into Leopoldville 19 *Ilyushin* aircraft packed with Soviet and Czech arms, and the CIA was now out to get him.

The day I arrived in the Congo, things began to go badly for the Soviets and their champion Patrice Lumumba. On that day, the United Nations, with the backing of Western intelligence agencies, had raised enough funds to pay the wages arrears of the mutinous Congolese Army which had driven out its Belgian officers and had not been paid since then.

That night, I toured the bars of the African quarter with a col-league to find them full of drunken Congolese soldiers praising Joseph Mobutu, their commander, for their payout. Mobutu a former clerk in the *Force Publique*, went on to become President Mobutu Sesse Seko – one of the richest and most corrupt men in Africa.

Emboldened by his sudden popularity with his troops, Mobutu announced his takeover of the government, closed down the Soviet and Czech embassies and demanded the withdrawal of the pro-Soviet Ghana and Guinea contingents of the UN forces in the Congo.

It was a considerable coup for the American and British intelli-gence services working jointly to frustrate Soviet plans for Africa. One of the most active and effective figures on the Leopoldville scene at the time was the formidable Daphne Park, the MI6 agent who made her reputation in the Congo. She was to be seen every-where, a full, ample-bosomed figure who, seemed to know all the Congolese leaders and clearly played a leading role in the intelli-gence war.

A huge press corps poured into Leopoldville and tried to make sense of all the confusion. At the time of my arrival three Congolese leaders – Lumumba, Mobutu and Joseph Kasavubu – all claimed to be in charge of the government and all held constant press confer-ences to assert their claims. Covering these entailed crossing checkpoints manned by trigger-happy soldiers. 'What do you call a drunken Congolese soldier, with steel helmet and dark glasses push-ing a Kalashnikov into your stomach?' Answer: 'Monsieur!'

Hardly less fearsome were the white mercenaries nicknamed *Les Affreux*, 'the frightful ones', bearded, festooned with daggers and grenades, who officered the various private armies that sprang up after independence. Outside the capital tribal fighting raged, totally beyond the control of the thinly-stretched UN forces, some of whom were devoured by local cannibals.

'Died in the Bush'

The press were working about 20 hours a day, largely due to an instrument of torture – the Leopoldville telex office. The telex was the only way of getting stories out unless you crossed the Congo river into Brazzaville and risked not being able to return. But the temperature of the telex office around midday was well over a hundred degrees Fahrenheit and there were just four telex lines, which only worked from time to time. A small Congolese telex clerk, smelly pipe clenched in his mouth, constantly scooted around the office seated on a wheeled typist's chair with a list of 50 or so correspondents desperately trying to file their stories.

As he trundled by, we would thrust large sums of money at him as bribes to get our calls through, until his pockets were bulging with bank notes. In these conditions we would wait, our necks wreathed in telex tape, as much as 15 hours to get a line – and then sometimes the machine would chatter and die just as you began to get through.

While we sweated and waited, the situation outside would change out of all recognition – Lumumba would be arrested, Lumumba would escape and give a press conference, Mobutu would announce a takeover, or troops would open fire in the streets. Excited reporters would rush in with accounts of the latest dramas, while those waiting desperately tried to change their leads before their calls came through.

With a thriving currency black market selling Congolese francs at a sixth of the official rate, the foreign press had never been so rich. One correspondent's wife rather gave the show away when she managed to get through to her husband on the newspaper's telex which circulates copies of all telex messages. 'Thanks for the traveller's cheques, darling,' she said somewhat naively. 'I've bought the washing-machine, shall I go ahead and buy the car?'

Passing through the capital of Katanga, Elizabethville (now Lubumbashi), several months later, during a period of comparative quiet, I was surprised to see correspondents hammering away at all the available telexes. Alarmed, I asked if a big story had just broken.

'No, nothing is happening, they are just onto their brokers,' I was told.

Covering the Congo story from Elizabethville involved frequent money runs across the border into Northern Rhodesia (now Zambia) to carry out copy to beat the censorship and collect traveller's cheques or currency from Barclays Bank. This entailed very hairy trips along a muram road to the Copper Belt, carrying cigarettes and money as bribes for the Katangese Gendarmerie, who were no less frightening than their opposite numbers in Leopoldville.

To make matters worse the expedition sometimes came under fire from UN troops – Nigerians, Indians, Swedes – who added their contribution to the chaos in their efforts to end the secession of Katanga, the one region in the Congo where there had been some semblance of law and order. Having run this gauntlet, it was a curious experience to find oneself suddenly in another world, such as Kitwe or Ndola on a Saturday afternoon where white Rhodesian couples with children in prams sat in cafés or went about their weekend shopping.

On one journey back to Elizabethville the *Daily Mail*'s Peter Younghusband and John Monks of the *Daily Express* found a newly arrived *Baltimore Sun* correspondent and a CBS cameraman being beaten close to death by a group of intoxicated Katangese troops at the border post. Younghusband, who tried to interfere, was also knocked down with a rifle butt and beaten. The two Americans were then stripped to their shorts and lined up against a wall to be shot. They were saved by a Katangese officer who arrived just in time to prevent the executions. When the group got back to Kitwe the *Baltimore Sun* reporter was in bad shape and had to be heavily sedated.

Younghusband and Monks filed their stories and then suddenly realised that their American colleague was about to miss probably the best story of his career. Feeling sorry for him, in best Fleet Street style, they wrote a sizzling story in his name and sent it to his paper. The *Baltimore Sun* splashed it, it was run by agencies in papers around the world and was even nominated for a Pulitzer.

Katanga became increasingly the focus of the Congo story as UN troops battled with the forces of Katanga's President Moise Tshombe to end secession. Tshombe had more style than his Leopoldville colleagues and only served the best champagne at his press conferences. In the midst of all this UN Secretary General Dag Hammarskjöld flew out for talks with Tshombe but was killed when his plane crashed in Rhodesia in mysterious circumstances.

Some time before this, I attended a chilling press conference in

which Tshombe's sinister, ice-cold Interior Minister Godefroid
Munongo announced Lumumba's death. Munongo, in his dark
glasses, looking like a bogeyman or a Ton Ton Macout, told us that
Lumumba had escaped from custody and had been killed by villagers. He then showed us the death certificate which stated simply
'died in the bush'. 'There are people who accuse us of assassination,'
he said. 'I have only one response – prove it.'

In fact, Lumumba had been flown under arrest to Elizabethville
and had been beaten almost senseless on the flight. Munongo, who
had been waiting for him on arrival, seized a bayonet from one of his
soldiers and plunged it repeatedly into Lumumba's heart. An Indian
newspaper correspondent said he had been told that Lumumba was
later partly eaten by his enemies and that 'his fingers were served as
canapés.' It was the sort of story one would normally be inclined to
disregard; in the Congo I am not so sure.

In the midst of my Congo coverage for the *Chronicle* I went for a
brief break with some colleagues to Salisbury (now Harare) in what
was then Southern Rhodesia. We had just arrived at the hotel and I
was having a drink in the early evening with a group of British and
American correspondents when I was called to the phone. 'Is that Mr
Beeston?' said a cockney voice. ' I've been told to tell you not to file
tonight. The paper's just folded.'

5

London

The Minister's Thumb

We held a rather boozy wake for the *News Chronicle* in Salisbury. At one stage I remember someone pouring a glass of beer over the head of the ITN correspondent Reggie Bosanquet which, to everyone's surprise, detached an unsuspected toupée.

My colleagues were exceedingly sympathetic. But for some reason I did not feel particularly concerned about the future; in fact, after months of rumours, the *Chronicle*'s final demise came almost as a relief.

I went back to Beirut to start packing up the flat and then returned to London to look for a job. But it was a bad year for Beeston fortunes. Just as the *Chronicle* folded Moyra's job had also rather dramatically collapsed.

She had been responsible for producing a daily English Hour programme on Beirut Radio, sponsored by the British Embassy. It included interviews, a music request programme and a news bulletin. Sunday was a day off with the hour filled with a taped play purchased from the BBC.

One Sunday, the play was billed as a drama about a farming family and disputes between the generations. What the précis on the recording did not mention was that the family was Jewish and that the farmer was advising his son to carve out a farm for himself in Palestine. Moyra handed the recording to the Lebanese studio engineer and then we all went off happily for a family picnic in the Krak des Chevaliers in Syria. A nasty diplomatic incident followed with the pro-Nasser Lebanese press attacking the British Embassy for spreading Israeli propaganda. An embarrassed Lebanese government then closed down the programme and Moyra was out of a job.

61

A friend of ours, Mai Jumblatt, the wife of the Lebanese Druze leader, was sympathetic and arranged for Moyra to meet her uncle, the Lebanese Minister of Information. The rendezvous was fixed for morning coffee at the appropriately named Diplomat Café where Moyra was to appeal for the government to cancel its ban. 'What shall I say to him?' Moyra asked uneasily before leaving. 'Tell him you have an unemployed husband and two children to support,' I suggested helpfully.

But fortune was not on our side. On alighting from his limousine, the minister trapped his thumb in the car door. Moyra, Mai and the minister sat down in the café, with the minister's six armed body-guards at the next table. However, he showed far more interest in his swollen thumb, wrapped up in his handkerchief and laid out accusingly on the café table, than in the future of Moyra's career in broadcasting. The English Hour stayed closed.

When I arrived in London, Fleet Street was still in a state of shock over the *Chronicle*'s collapse. There was a lot of affection for the *Chronicle*, or the 'newspaperman's newspaper' as it was known, but there was a limit to the number of *Chronicle* journalists the other papers could absorb – and arriving late I was last in line.

The liberal *News Chronicle* had been bought out by Lord Rothermere of Associated Newspapers, for an improbable merger with the right-wing *Daily Mail*. Sacrificed along with the *Chronicle* was its successful evening paper stable-mate, the *Star*. The real purpose of the deal was to eliminate competition. For a very short time the *Chronicle*'s title was carried below the *Mail*'s masthead and a number of *Chronicle* staff taken on by the *Mail* transformed it into a rather more liberal publication.

This soon ended, however. The *Mail* reverted to its far-right ideology, consequently retaining only a small share of the *Chronicle*'s 1.2 million daily circulation. It was a seedy manoeuvre by the chocolate millionaire Laurence Cadbury, who had made no real effort to save the *Chronicle* or offer it to other buyers. The justification for the deal was to pay off the *Chronicle*'s debts and provide proper compensation for the staff. A year or so later I did receive compensation from the Cadbury family. It was a cheque accompanied by a letter that warned that if I were unaccustomed to handling such a large sum of money, I should place it in a bank or a building society. The cheque was for £200.

Doing the rounds of Fleet Street I finally turned up in the office of SR Pawley, an avuncular figure known fondly as 'Pop' and managing editor of *The Daily Telegraph*. The *Telegraph* had already taken on a dozen or so *Chronicle* journalists so I did not hold much hope of landing a job there. 'We've been waiting for you Beeston,' said Pop Pawley, much to my surprise. 'Ian Colvin says you are a good man and we should have you on the paper, so I am holding a job for you if you want it.'

Ian Colvin was the *Telegraph*'s Middle East correspondent and his apartment had been exactly opposite mine in Beirut. He was very hard-working, and from my window I could regularly see him typing away. Often after returning from skiing or a picnic I would call him up to see if there was any news to file, and he would cheerfully fill me in. It is really to Ian that I owe 26 very agreeable years with the *Telegraph*.

Only about a fortnight after joining the *Telegraph* I found myself once more back in the Congo. Different paper – same story.

Port in a Storm

After the traumas of the last years of the *Chronicle* I had, by luck, switched to Fleet Street's most stable newspaper. The *Telegraph* seemed to have hit on a magic formula, with a circulation three or four times that of *The Times* and the *Guardian*, a solid, prosperous middle-class readership and plenty of advertising.

The pride of the *Telegraph* was its domestic and foreign hard news coverage. Abroad, the *Telegraph* correspondent was usually the first on the scene on a news story and the last to leave, and the paper had the largest corps of foreign correspondents of the British press.

Despite its far-right political slant, stories were judged on their hard news value, while within the *Telegraph*'s grey, austere columns lurked the most lurid and salacious scourings from the courts that often the tabloids declined to print.

Our readers seemed undeterred by the ludicrous, hidebound restraints imposed by the *Telegraph* 'house-style' which involved writing in a permanent straightjacket – two short sentences to a paragraph and any attempt at humour or irony ruthlessly censored out by the subs. Any reference to a boat or ship, from a small launch to a supertanker, had to be followed by its tonnage, whatever its relevance. Any dollar figure had to be translated into sterling. An hilarious example of this rule appears in Duff Hart-Davis's book *The House the Berrys Built* which quotes Elizabeth Taylor in a Telegraph report as saying 'I'm feeling like a million dollars (£357,000)'.

Features on the whole were boring and predictable, with the main feature article standing out like a tombstone on the editorial page.

The editorials themselves usually reflected the dotty, eccentric views of the Tory far right – but, oddly, the reporters were mostly left wing.

Life at 135 Fleet Street, I quickly discovered, had much in common with my experience of an infantry battalion, incorporating many of the army's very English snobberies and class distinctions. There was also more than a touch of feudal England about the *Telegraph*.

Our CO, or Lord-of-the-Manor, was the Honourable Michael Berry, the paper's owner and editor-in-chief. Few people ever met him, but throughout the building he was referred to, with awe, as 'Mr Michael'. His merest whim or prejudice, perhaps expressed with no more than a frown or a sigh, for he was a man of few words, was immediately passed down through the ranks, and wherever possible reflected somewhere in the columns of his newspaper.

Mr Michael's command post, or seat, was established on the fifth floor and 'The Fifth Floor' became a term that commanded almost religious respect. As befitting a stately home, the Fifth Floor boasted a butler, a chef, even a gardener who tended a small lawn and flower beds high above Fleet Street, a library, a suite of panelled rooms and a dining room where once a week selected members of the staff lunched uneasily.

George Evans, the assistant editor of *The Sunday Telegraph* who frequently sent me out on foreign stories, would often remark in hushed tones that my assignment had originated from 'up there' as he cast his eyes reverentially heavenwards to the fifth floor rather than daring to name the source or even the location of the directive.

As in a battalion, the staff of *The Daily Telegraph* were divided fairly clearly into officers and other ranks. In my first post I seemed to have a foot in both camps. I was the paper's fireman – ready to rush off at a moment's notice to some Third World disaster not staffed by a resident correspondent. Immediately on returning from these trips, however, I was placed firmly in the newsroom covering local stories, the weather or writing obituaries until the next coup or civil war. The newsroom was definitely 'other ranks' with reporters working through the News Editor, the Night Editor and the Managing Editor but rarely catching sight of the Editor and least of all the Editor-in-Chief.

The atmosphere at the *Telegraph* was much less relaxed than it had been at the *Chronicle*. I caused raised eyebrows on my first day in the newsroom, when I strolled into the Editor's office to introduce myself to Sir Colin Coote, an amiable but somewhat aloof and patrician figure. Appearances were, however, deceptive. In fact, in his earlier life, Coote could have made rather a good romantic hero in a Hollywood movie.

At one time, he raced at Brooklands and as a dashing infantry officer in the First World War he met and fell in love with a young Frenchwoman in a war zone. Later, believing reports that she had been killed in a bombardment, he married an English girl. Several years later, he arrived at Brown's Hotel with his wife and children. As he was signing the register in walked the French girlfriend. After a passionate embrace, abandoning his family, he promptly walked out of the hotel with her and they were eventually married.

Another of Sir Colin's claims to fame, or notoriety, was his inadvertent role in the Christine Keeler scandal which led to the resignation of Sir Harold Macmillan. It was Sir Colin who introduced Stephen Ward, his osteopath, to the Soviet Naval Attaché Eugene Ivanov. Ward then brought together that explosive mixture, Christine, Ivanov and the Secretary of State for War John Profumo.

Sir Colin's job as Editor was a good deal less stressful than that of most of his colleagues in Fleet Street. Under a divide-and-rule system, the editor was only really responsible for the editorial pages and had his own staff of editorial writers. The day-to-day running of the paper, the news coverage, hiring and firing, and putting the paper to bed was the responsibility of the Managing Editor.

Again in military analogy the Editor was a sort of battalion second-in-command while the rough tasks were handled for the CO by the Managing Editor, or Regimental Sergeant Major. Under Pop Pawley this system worked fairly benignly, but tensions between the Editor and Managing Editor became far more pronounced when Pawley retired to be replaced by a more fearsome figure, the ambitious and unpredictable Night Editor Peter Eastwood.

Life at the 'King and Keys'

A very different sort of editor from the somewhat Olympian personality of Colin Coote was Bill Deedes, Evelyn Waugh's model for William Boot, his hero in *Scoop*.

Deedes was first encountered by Waugh on Addis Ababa railway station, where he had just arrived with a mountain of baggage from Austin Reed to cover the Abyssinian war for The *Morning Post*.

Even as editor of the *Telegraph* for over a decade, Bill Deedes maintained the enthusiasm and excitement of the young reporter that Waugh had met. Once, when I was in a bar in Dallas with Bill and a number of other correspondents, covering a Republican presidential election convention, we heard some fire engines screaming past. Bill could never resist a fire engine and it was our elderly editor who led the pack down the street in pursuit of the fire.

He much preferred being out on a story, but as editor he was always charming, informal, in shirt-sleeves and available for a drink in his office or a visit to the pub next door. He became the bibulous 'Dear Bill' character in *Private Eye* through his friendship with Denis Thatcher. He had a 'shurly' slurring of speech easy to take off, and was often mistaken for another former *Telegraph* employee, Malcolm Muggeridge.

But for all his informality, Bill was quite a grandee, once a government minister, who eventually became a peer. His appointment in the 1970s raised hopes that the new Editor would stand up more to the Managing Editor, especially on behalf of staff being unfairly persecuted. Peter Eastwood's behaviour was becoming more eccentric and his growing reputation as the Genghis Khan of the *Telegraph* was spreading a lot of misery around the paper. However, the staff waited in vain for a confrontation between Editor and Managing Editor. Deedes played by the Hartwell rules and the RSM was left in command of an increasingly unhappy paper.

Most of the staff fell foul of Eastwood at some stage. I attribute my own success in avoiding this fate by remaining several thousand miles away from Fleet Street throughout his reign and by placing my wife strategically between myself and Peter during our annual lunches with him in London.

Michael Berry, who was to become Lord Hartwell, incorporated the old-fashioned virtues of hard work, honesty and thrift. He was tall, dark and handsome, self-effacing, embarrassingly shy and very stubborn. This last characteristic contributed to his loss of control of the *Telegraph* to the Canadian, Conrad Black, in 1986.

When his father, Lord Camrose, died in 1954, it was widely assumed that Michael Berry's elder and more worldly brother, Seymour, who inherited the title, would take over. But Seymour, a racier character who drank a lot, was made Chairman. It was Michael who was handed the responsibility of running the paper, which he did, night and day, for over 30 years, the only hands-on owner in Fleet Street to physically edit his paper. He was, according to Bill Deedes, 'the last proprietor for whom profit was not a serious consideration. Reputation was all.' Seymour, meanwhile, was rarely seen around. He spent much of his time in the Mediterranean aboard his yacht with Joan Guinness, the former wife of Aly Khan. Their friends referred to the couple as 'the boat people.'

Lord Hartwell's only real innovation during his long reign was his bold decision to launch *The Sunday Telegraph* at a seemingly unpropitious time when *The Sunday Times* and *The Observer* appeared to have cornered the market. The Camrose formula in the 1930s which Hartwell inherited and maintained, entailed concise editing to cram as much news as possible into the paper with two sentences to a paragraph and few news stories exceeding 400 words. Hartwell's chief interest was hard news and consequently the features pages of the *Telegraph* were the weakest part of the paper.

In the early 1980s, during an endless and costly struggle with the printing unions, the *Telegraph* began to encounter serious financial problems while Hartwell was spending a fortune on the new plant in Canary Wharf to bring in the new technology. He lacked the toughness of Rupert Murdoch, and things grew worse until it became clear that Lord Hartwell was failing to remedy the problems of the paper and its ageing readership. Badly in need of money to finance the modernisation plans, Hartwell borrowed an initial loan from the Canadian millionaire Conrad Black, which eventually enabled Black to seize a controlling share.

On my last visit to the Fifth Floor, workmen were gutting the building in preparation for the move to the Isle of Dogs. Amidst the drilling and sawing, Hartwell, isolated and outwitted by the new regime, was still at his desk, but already cut off from the running of the paper and stripped of his editorial powers. It was an undignified end of an era in which he had run, for so long, two of Britain's most successful papers and inaugurated the technology which was to restore their fortunes.

But these were distant days hence from the time I joined the *Telegraph* when it was at the peak of its success. In those times, however, despite the air of Victorian respectability that surrounded the *Telegraph*, there was something almost Hogarthian about the uninhibited antics of the staff at the 'King and Keys' next door. Here, senior members of Hartwell's staff passed rumbustious nights while their colleagues from the flashier papers were at home in Bromley drinking cocoa with their wives.

The focus of the heavy drinking and rowdyism which occasionally ended in a punch-up was a depressing little corridor of a pub right next door to the *Telegraph*. Here editorial and specialist writers would drink and quarrel – often dangerously spilling out across Fleet Street to the pub opposite, the 'Falstaff' – sometimes at cost to life or limb.

The 'King and Keys' was entered late at night at one's peril, not least the risk of exposure to a verbal lashing from a senior correspondent who worked resolutely to maintain his reputation as being the rudest man in Fleet Street. On being introduced to a friend of mine who had just joined the *Telegraph*, he looked at him, scowled and remarked 'remind me, I can't remember which of you is queer, you or your brother.'

The atmosphere of a rowdy bohemianism of another era was nicely described by Michael Wharton, a regular at the pub who wrote the Peter Simple Column for the *Telegraph*, in his brilliant autobiography *A Dubious Codicil.* He describes our correspondent's performance as the centrepiece of a drunken 'Theatre of the Absurd' that was played out nightly. A typical evening was when Peregrine Worsthorne, who later became Editor of *The Sunday Telegraph*, came in for a quiet drink. 'You're a phony,' he croaked. 'You're a hollow man. You're a tinsel king on a cardboard throne.'

Among other regulars at 'the Keys' were Colin Welch the *Telegraph*'s Deputy Editor and Peter Utley, the *Telegraph*'s blind, very bright, very right-wing leader writer. Despite his handicap, Utley was an object of much envy by the staff. I never went into 'the Keys' without seeing Utley, a piratical patch over one of his eyes, sitting at a table with at least a couple of extremely attractive and entirely devoted young women.

When *The Sunday Telegraph* was started, shortly after I joined, the editor Donald McLachlan, who had the air of a slightly mad professor, had a bright idea and summoned Peter Utley to his office. 'How would you feel about being our television correspondent?' he asked. 'But Donald, haven't you overlooked something?' spluttered Utley, jabbing his white stick on the floor.

Luncheon on the Fifth Floor

There was no greater contrast to the boisterous atmosphere of 'the Keys' than being summoned to the Fifth Floor for luncheon with Lord Hartwell. There was a strict rule of one drink before being seated in his dining room, where each of the guests had a white pad of paper and a ferociously sharpened pencil next to his bread plate. I could never think of anything to write on my pad, but I noticed they would all be collected after lunch and wondered if there would be some sort of post-mortem to identify the notes, squiggles and doodling carried out during some quite frequent and daunting gaps in the conversation.

Lord Hartwell was very good at gaps, whether through shyness or design. But they were inclined to make one burble on, in a desperate attempt to fill them, and thereby often exposing the emptiness of one's views or knowledge of the subject under discussion. Such disclosures would not go unobserved. On home leave I would normally see Lord Hartwell in his office and would save up a few local anecdotes or gossip from my posting abroad to last me out.

Occasionally he opened up with his own stories. Once when we were on the subject of Burgess and MacLean he told me of the time that Guy Burgess contacted Hartwell to see if he could get a job. Burgess was in disgrace, just having been thrown out of his post with the British Embassy in Washington. Lord Hartwell, who knew Burgess fairly well, asked him round to dinner and invited a mutual acquaintance Anthony Blunt.

Burgess, however, failed to show up, and as the evening progressed, Lord Hartwell told me, Blunt became increasingly uneasy. Hartwell finally phoned up Burgess's club to be told 'He seems to have disappeared, Sir.' Blunt, clearly a worried man, left the Hartwells early, on what turned out to be the night of the two spies' defection.

One *Telegraph* special writer turned up very drunk to a Hartwell lunch. As a result, in the best Victorian traditions, he was sent off to the colonies to be a correspondent in Africa.

I was based in Nairobi at the time, when my Foreign Editor Ricky Marsh came through on a secret mission. It emerged that our new correspondent in Salisbury had not filed a story for more than a fortnight and had holed up in his hotel room with a large number of bottles. It took Marsh a couple of days to persuade him to open his door and another day drinking with him until he could persuade him to come home. The *Telegraph* generously paid for him to be dried out, then put him straight back into the newsroom on weather and obits. where he almost immediately relapsed into alcoholism.

Fireman

When we returned to London from Beirut we bought a Victorian terrace house in Hammersmith, on the bend of the river, just right for Boat Race parties. However, working as a 'fireman' for the *Telegraph* and also the newly launched *Sunday Telegraph*, for the next three years I spent little time at home.

It was a schizophrenic sort of existence. Often I would set out for a dull day in the newsroom and later find myself phoning home from Heathrow en route to some remote spot in Africa or Asia I had barely heard of. 'There's a request for a story from up there,' George

Evans would say, eyes cast to the ceiling. 'We want you in Conakry by tonight and a story by tomorrow.'

Conakry? Sometimes without even a moment to check the place on a map I would rush out to the airport, buy copies of *Time*, *Newsweek* and *The Economist* and hope that one of them would tell me what was going on there. What had caught the proprietor's eye was a report that part of a consignment of Soviet economic aid to Conakry, capital of Guinea, had included snow ploughs. It turned out to be true!

Africa was big news in the 1960s and the next story I covered after the Congo was the horrific uprising against the Portuguese in Angola. The massacre of a thousand whites and mulattos came as a total surprise to the Portuguese and was the beginning of the collapse of Portugal's huge, slumbering empire in Africa. The uprising was a direct result of the events in neighbouring Congo and was planned from there by Angolan exiles. But although the consequences were even bloodier, Angola never had the same impact on the world press as the Congo.

When I arrived in Luanda there were only about 1,500 Portuguese troops in the entire territory and reinforcements were being rushed in to bring the numbers up to 50,000. The Portuguese prided themselves that Angola was a non-racist society and encouraged inter-marriage between the 200,000 largely peasant Portuguese white settlers and the blacks, although in almost every case it was a Portuguese man marrying a black woman. The policy was also to give full rights of citizenship to the *assimilados* – a very small percentage indeed of blacks who had achieved some form of education, largely from missionary schools.

However, since these were the ones who were politicised, it was the literate blacks who were hunted down by revenge-seeking settlers and who were eliminated in their thousands by *PIDE*, the Portuguese secret police. As far as *PIDE* was concerned, every African who could read or write was considered to be an enemy and their wholesale slaughter fanned the racial flames.

There was a ban on the foreign press entering Angola, but for some reason they let me in. This was possibly because of the good Tory credentials of the *Telegraph* or because our editor Sir Colin Coote happened to be a personal friend – I imagine one of the very few – of Portugal's dictator Antonio de Oliviera Salazar.

The military flew me in a helicopter over large areas of Northern Angola where most of the roads were blocked with felled trees, villages had been burned down and Portuguese farms under siege. In Luanda, armed civilians were hunting down terrorist suspects and

once, when having a coffee in an open-air café, a black Angolan was
chased to the top of a building by a white mob, hurled from the roof
and landed on the pavement beside me.

In the worst trouble spots the rebels burned down entire towns,
killing with *pangas* any white or mulatto they could find. Rebel-
occupied towns were in turn bombed and strafed by the Portuguese
airforce and survivors finished off by paratroopers. Angola's thick
jungle and mountainous terrain provided perfect conditions for
rebel operations. About 70 miles of the Angola–Congo frontier were
in the hands of the rebels and this was the supply route for the rebels'
small arms and machine-guns.

Searching for a scapegoat to blame for an uprising which took them
completely by surprise, the Angolan authorities picked on the
Protestant missions, and white crowds attacked British and American
mission headquarters in Luanda. There, the massive sixteenth-century
Portuguese fortress of St Miguel which dominates the harbour, was
being converted when I arrived from a museum to a barracks for
hundreds of paras pouring in from Portugal.

One of the reasons for the build-up of racial tensions, which cul-
minated in March 1961 in the massacre of hundreds of Portuguese
men, women and children, was the dumping there of Portugal's sur-
plus poor white population who were competing with Africans on
unequal terms for even the lowest level jobs.

Angola was even less prepared than the former Belgian Congo
for independence. But to most people, except the Portuguese (and
probably my editor!) the outcome seemed inevitable. The revolt
marked the beginning of the end of the Portuguese empire. Finally,
Portugal was forced to give up its African possessions in Angola and
Mozambique – which both then proceeded to slip into civil war and
anarchy.

My minder during my travels in Angola was a pleasant young
Portuguese Navy Commander. However, our relationship became
increasingly strained as I managed to sneak out some uncensored stories about how bad things really were. He became particularly
agitated when he heard from Lisbon that they had read my reports of
the Portuguese Army practice of leaving piles of severed heads of
rebels stuck on poles, stacked up by the roadside. The Army made no
bones about its reason for this. Witch doctors had told the rebels they
would return to life if killed in an attack on the whites, and the Army
believed that the grisly sight of their comrades' severed heads would
destroy this myth.

Somehow, the Commander had the impression that I had

reported that the Army had been cutting off heads from living bodies for this purpose. When I explained that I had only stated that the heads had been hacked from the bodies of dead rebels, he seemed surprisingly reassured. But I could see that my time was running out and shortly afterwards I was politely informed that my visa was not being renewed.

Returning to Fleet Street after such assignments always came as a shock. After one longish period in tropical Africa I found myself, the morning after my return, standing on a freezing pavement with a group of other reporters covering an eviction in Wandsworth.

There was a Dickensian schoolroom air about the newsroom where grown men, some into their middle age, would sit at desks facing the News Editor and his two assistants, waiting around for something to happen. The specialists in say, education, property or medical services usually found something to do. But the general reporters, or someone like myself who knew nothing about home reporting, were desperately bored and underemployed. I sometimes felt like volunteering to go and cut Lord Hartwell's lawn on the Fifth Floor!

Covering an uprising in Africa or a coup in the Middle East was infinitely preferable, along with a bunch of colleagues like myself who never really grew up. On a major foreign story, there was never anything like the blanket press coverage that came with television news, and I suppose started with the Vietnam War.

Competition was not nearly so serious abroad, and inevitably there was a great sense of comradeship among the reporters and photographers who regularly covered the world's hot spots. Well-known foreign correspondents of the 1950s and 1960s had the sort of recognition and fame enjoyed by star television reporters today. Evelyn Waugh's description in *Scoop* of Wenlock Jakes, the syndicated correspondent who overslept in his railway carriage on his way to cover a Balkan revolution, woke up in the wrong capital and had a revolution there going in no time at all, was not such a wild flight of fantasy.

The *Daily Express*'s René McColl could well have done it, or his *Daily Mail* rival Noel Barber. At the time of the Chinese invasion of Tibet a group of correspondents which included Barber chartered an aircraft from India that was turned back at the Tibetan border by the Indian Air Force. As a disconsolate group of reporters alighted from the plane Barber announced cheerfully that he had already filed his story before take-off. The next day the *Mail* carried an eye-witness description from Barber of the Dalai Lama on horseback leading his monks through a mountain pass with his blazing palace in the background.

Sefton Delmer of the *Express* was still a big name at that period. He used to tell the story of an earlier time when he covered the *Reichstag* fire. Filing his story from Berlin he described vividly how he had walked beside Adolf Hitler through the smouldering ruins of the Reichstag. Having dictated the story, surely one of the most dramatic of the century, he asked the news telephonist if there were any queries. ''Ang on Mr Delmer, I'll ask the news desk.' Long pause. 'The night editor wants to know how many fire appliances there were at the scene.'

After the war, Delmer, who looked like a German, dressed himself up as a typical German tourist and visited a cemetery in Normandy containing the graves of many members of the French resistance who had been executed by the Nazis. The French custodian of the cemetery, he reported, was exceedingly polite. The Second World War, he told Delmer, had been an unfortunate episode, but of course it was the English who were France's real enemies.

The *Daily Mirror*'s Don Wise was one of the more amusing and eccentric members of the foreign press corps of the 1960s. He spent most of the war as a prisoner of the Japanese and put on little weight afterwards. An ex-paratrooper, tall, thin and elegant, with a small military moustache, Don, who had also been a rubber planter in Malaya, improbably spent part of the post-war emergency there in charge of a group of headhunters pursuing communist Chinese rebels.

In one memorable despatch from Vietnam during Buddhist clashes with the Saigon government, Don described how, after a day of unrest, peace descended on the city, disturbed only by the sound of truncheons 'descending on the shaven heads of saffron-clad Buddhist monks as they helped the police with their investigations.'

John Ridley, a *Telegraph* colleague, was another of the foreign press regulars. He was slight and completely fearless. For some reason he would be left out on a limb, for long periods in obscure parts of the world, well after interest in the story had evaporated. Rather than complain, he used to fine the *Telegraph* by upping his expenses.

At one time, he found himself stuck on the island of Quemoy, under regular shelling from the Chinese mainland. Each evening he would report faithfully on how many shells had fallen on Quemoy during the day. Finally, even the *Telegraph* became bored with the story and cabled John rather petulantly 'How much longer is this going on?' 'How should I know?' cabled back an exasperated Ridley, 'My balls aren't made of crystal.' In response to this John received a rather huffy letter from the Managing Editor which stated 'Dear Mr Ridley, kindly keep obscenities out of your cables as they often pass through the hands of young, unmarried girls'.

Under Curfew

A story about corruption and graft in West Africa, Lord Hartwell told George Evans, might be interesting. So I was duly despatched – and it was not hard to find. I ended up in Accra in 1961 and made several trips there over the next few months.

On one occasion I arrived only a week or so before a controversial scheduled visit to Ghana by Queen Elizabeth and Prince Philip. Ghana was in crisis, most of the opposition were locked up, and the opponents of 'President for Life' Kwame Nkrumah saw the royal visit as an endorsement of his repressive policies.

Ghana, the former British colony of the Gold Coast, became in 1957 one of the first British territories in Africa to gain independence. When it was handed over it was one of the most prosperous nations in Africa with strong financial reserves, a well-educated population and an efficient civil service. But by the time Nkrumah was overthrown, like so many newly independent states who were to follow the same road, Ghana was a wreck and ripe for a succession of military coups.

After a very short time there I gained the impression that opposition to Nkrumah's dictatorship had reached boiling point and wrote a piece for the *Telegraph* warning of possible security risks to the Queen's visit. Hearing that this warning had been taken seriously in London and that the visit was now under review I felt somewhat uneasy that I might have overstated the security threat.

It was, therefore, I have to admit, with a feeling of some relief that in the early hours of the morning five days before the visit I was awakened by two large explosions. One was near the route of the royal visit. The other was beside a life-size statue of Nkrumah outside parliament which bore the inscription 'Seek ye first the political kingdom and all other things shall be added unto it'. For Nkrumah, the inscription could not have been better phrased.

More bombs went off and Commonwealth Secretary Duncan Sandys, with men from Scotland Yard, flew in to assess the situation. Finally, it was decided that the visit should go ahead. Prime Minister Harold Macmillan told parliament that, although the Queen's safety weighed most with him, it would not be right to disregard the wider implications 'including the forward movement of the Commonwealth'.

The visit went off without incident, but it did nothing to assuage Nkrumah's growing and paranoid hatred of Britain and the West and his clear preference for the communist bloc. In Ghana, the movement of the Commonwealth was clearly going in the other direction.

In the four years since independence, Nkrumah had squandered most of his country's resources, largely to further his pan-African ambitions, and had crushed all political opposition. As the royal couple arrived, political refugees were flooding into neighbouring Togo. On a visit to a hospital in Accra, Prince Philip was photographed speaking to a young patient, the son of an imprisoned opposition leader. 'When did you last see your father?' was a caption that appeared in the British press.

Anti-British feeling among the regime continued to build up, and when I arrived back in Accra the following year on a long Britannia flight from London, I was immediately picked up when I reached my hotel by a pleasant immigration officer. 'I have special instructions to expel you on the first plane out of Accra,' he said. So I was put aboard the Britannia aircraft on which I had arrived, and was back in London two days after my departure.

Two weeks later I slipped back in from Lagos. The Ghana authorities had just declared a state of emergency and a curfew, and troops were ransacking the homes of hundreds of suspected critics of Nkrumah, beating them up in the streets before throwing them into prison. A fortnight later I was expelled again following a communist-directed Ghana press and radio campaign against the British press. In the Ghana evening news on the day of my departure we were described as 'disreputable Imperialist adventurers of Fleet St. capable of the worst type of crime the human brain can contrive'.

At about that time I found myself covering another *Telegraph* special in a more remote part of West Africa – the British Cameroons. Britain was pulling out from the territory, leaving behind some uneasy British farmers without protection from a local guerrilla force in the area.

To complete my story, I needed to interview the former prime minister, now leader of the opposition, who had decided to make himself scarce and had taken off into the bush. In the capital, Buea, I found an elderly black with an ancient taxi who claimed he could find my man, but whose driving was certainly eccentric.

We set out down a road which quickly became a narrow jungle track. At each incline, instead of putting on speed, he would bring the taxi to a dead stop, then put it into first gear and crawl up the hill. Progress was slow and evening was coming on when we had a puncture. I then discovered that there was no spare wheel – but undeterred, the driver plunged into the bush and began tearing up the tall grass to fill the punctured tyre.

I began to be resigned to a night in the jungle when down the deserted track came a Land Rover heading for the capital. The large, rather jolly Cameroonian driver who offered me a lift back turned out, to my delight, to be the very man I was seeking. We drove off along the track, but just as I reached for my pencil and notebook for my interview I was hit in the stomach by a most horrific stench. It was, my companion explained cheerfully, from the remains of an ele-phant in the back which he had shot several days before. I found the only way I could avoid being sick on the spot was to hang my head out of the land rover, as far as possible while avoiding the vegetation, and travelled in this way until we finally reached the outskirts of town, where he dropped me off and sped away. Long after a shower and a change of clothes the smell of the elephant clung to me – and I never did get my interview.

My next assignment, in 1962, was to Oran to cover the three-cornered battles going on there between the OAS (*Organisation Armeé Secrète*) – the European settlers' secret army – the Moslems and the French security forces during the tense period leading to Algerian independence. The rules roughly were that the OAS ran the city at night, except for the Moslem areas, and the French forces ran it by day. But the situation became worse, and I witnessed the first pitched battles for Oran between the French arm and the OAS while the local European population from their balconies banged out on their saucepans and frying pans the five notes '*Al–ger–ie Fran–çaise*'.

During one battle, I was sheltering in the Hotel de Tourisme in Oran when a French Catholic priest ran up to an armoured car waving his arms and shouting to the crew 'Stop, you are shooting Frenchmen!' Inside the hotel, the manager, Oran's deputy mayor, dramatically tore from his lapel the *Légion d'honneur* won while serving in the French Army.

But the clashes seemed to mark the beginning of the end for the settlers' cause. The battles had exploded the myth that French sol-diers would never fire on Frenchmen, and a few days later the OAS suffered a shattering blow with the capture in Oran of General Jouhaud and his chief of operations. Jouhaud, an Algerian-born Frenchman and former Air Force General, was a hero in Oran and his voice was heard almost every night on an OAS pirate radio. Three months later it was all over, and Algeria became independent.

Tanks, armoured cars and rooftop snipers made news coverage in

Oran a dangerous business. The BBC correspondent believed he had solved the problem by striding through the streets in a bowler hat to demonstrate his neutrality. It seemed to work!

My *Telegraph* colleague in Algiers was our Paris correspondent John Wallace, irascible and never overly impressed by the odd goings-on of foreigners. On one occasion a terrifying group of OAS thugs armed with sub-machine-guns burst into the Aletti Hotel in Algiers in search of the Italian press which had been saying derogatory things about their Organisation. John was having a morning drink at the hotel bar, unmoved as everyone else hit the floor or took shelter under the tables. 'Where are the Italian journalists?' demanded the thugs pointing their guns at John. 'How the hell should I know?' he said turning round and glaring at them. 'Go and ask the Concierge.'

In the spring of 1963 I was sent out to Baghdad to cover the overthrow of Iraq's deranged dictator General Abdel Karim Kassem. Kassem was in the defence ministry when the military coup began. First he was bombed by the air force, then shelled by the army, and then troops broke through the defences and shot him.

In a macabre ending to the revolt, a Donald Duck cartoon on Baghdad television was suddenly interrupted and replaced by a shot of the nation's recently deceased president lolling back in his chair with a bullet wound through his head. Later, while having a drink at Baghdad's once exclusive Al Wiyah club, an outraged British businessman came up to me to complain about how sensational British newspaper coverage of the coup had upset his wife and family in England. I told him that even the British press would have trouble in sensationalising that story, but he seemed unconvinced.

As we poured into Iraq we were all confined to our hotel for about a week – under curfew, unable to send or receive cables or phone messages. When the curfew was finally relaxed a messenger came into the hotel loaded with old telegrams, usually beginning petulantly with 'WHY YOU UNFILED?'. One of my cables, five days old, came from Moyra to tell me that our son Richard had been born. But it was several weeks before I could get back to meet him.

Arabia not so Felix

My last assignment as The *Daily Telegraph*'s fireman took me to one of the world's most remote and beautiful spots – the high mountains of Northern Yemen.

Yemen, Arabia Felix of ancient times, is situated on the south-west tip of the Arabian peninsula. Land of the Queen of Sheba and of the

Incense Trail of frankincense and myrrh, it was once a great civilisation, centuries before Christ, and later became a remote and isolated outpost of the Ottoman Empire. Until the revolution of 1962 it was ruled as a theocracy by an Imam who was both king and spiritual leader and who enjoyed nothing more than stirring up trouble along the Aden border with the British.

The war in the Yemen in the 1960s, now a long forgotten event, was a fascinating microcosm of the post-Suez Middle East. It involved the rivalries between Nasser's Egypt and Saudi Arabia and the other traditionalist Gulf Arab States, the struggle for control of the region's oil riches, Britain's tenuous presence in the Arabian peninsula, and Anglo-American tensions in the region.

It also provided me with a rare scoop, when I was able to report that President Nasser could claim the distinction of being 'the first person to employ chemical warfare since Mussolini used mustard gas on Ethiopian tribesmen during the thirties'. Oddly enough, the next time poison gas was used in warfare was nearly 30 years later when President Saddam Hussein used it against his own population, and my son Richard was there to report it for *The Times* in the mountains of Iraqi Kurdistan.

In September 1962 Yemen's old tyrant, Imam Ahmad, much to everyone's surprise, died peacefully in his bed. Nearly all his predecessors had suffered more violent departures. His hapless successor was his weak and dissolute son Mohammed Al Badr, who had fallen under the spell of President Nasser and was bent on reforming his medieval kingdom.

But Nasser had his own plans. Al Badr's right-hand man and best friend was his chief of staff General Abdullah Sallal. He just happened to be Egypt's choice for heading a coup to transform Yemen into a pro-Egyptian puppet-republic.

For Nasser, the attraction of this conspiracy was that it would provide Egypt with a foothold in the Arabian peninsula, which contained most of the world's oil reserves. From there he would be positioned to subvert the Saudi Arabian monarchy and drive Britain out of Aden. Instead, Yemen proved a nightmare for Nasser, sucking him into a brutal and costly five-year war which became known as Egypt's 'Vietnam'.

One night, only a few days after he had come to power, the gullible new Imam found himself under bombardment in his palace in Sana and surrounded by tanks and troops commanded by his friend Abdullah Sallal. But as shells crashed through the top floor of the palace, Al Badr, showing unexpected initiative, slipped out through a back gate and escaped. Eventually he managed to reach the mountains to the north where the warrior Zeidi tribes, whose religious leader he was, rallied to the royalist cause.

Although the capital Sana and the other main towns fell to the rebels, it soon became clear that large areas of the north were entirely beyond the control of the central Government. Al Badr set up his military headquarters near the Saudi border while other princes established centres of resistance throughout the region.

The Yemeni coup occurred eight months after President Kennedy came to office. Britain and Saudi Arabia entreated Washington not to back the new puppet regime. Dana Adams Schmidt, the *New York Times* Middle East correspondent warned that Nasser's operation in Yemen – his 'biggest gamble' – was to reach far beyond Yemen 'to overthrow the monarchy of neighbouring Saudi Arabia and win control of that country's and other Arabian peninsula oil'. However, President Kennedy's 'New Frontiersmen' were out to prove that they were on the side of liberal, progressive elements in the world and would have no truck with reactionary, feudal monarchies. Three months after the coup the US gave full diplomatic recognition to the Sallal regime.

President Kennedy tried to persuade Harold Macmillan to follow suit. But Macmillan, strongly backed by Duncan Sandys, Secretary of State for Commonwealth Relations, and Julian Amery, Minister of Aviation, members of the so-called Aden Group, refused to do so. This decision proved extremely profitable. The Saudis were furious with the American recognition of the Yemeni Republic, with the result that Britain's policy ended an eight-year break in diplomatic relations with Saudi Arabia and opened up vast British arms sales to the Saudis who otherwise would have purchased them from their traditional allies, the Americans.

Once Al Badr had established his mountain headquarters, Saudi Arabia began sending arms across the border to the royalists. The failure of the Yemeni republicans to overcome royalist resistance eventually forced Egypt to send in a force of 60,000 troops, most of whom had never even seen a mountain, and a large section of the Egyptian Air Force which took to bombing Saudi frontier towns in an effort to stop the arms flow.

Everything Stops for *Qat*

In June 1963 I set out with an old colleague and friend, Joe Alex Morris of *Newsweek,* to visit the Imam's headquarters. Joe was an ideal companion. He was quite fearless, never lost his dry sense of humour and was remarkably patient with the frustrations of travelling in Arabia. It was his lack of fear that may have contributed to his death from a sniper's bullet in Teheran when his companions were wisely taking cover.

Setting out from Beirut, our first stop was Jeddah. The Saudi government was anxious to obtain publicity for the Yemeni royalists' struggle and agreed to back our trip. We then flew on to the Saudi Red Sea port of Jizan, close to the Yemeni border – one of the nastiest and hottest places in the world where the Saudi authorities deposited us in a concrete guest-house-cum-customs building to await our Yemeni escorts. The guest-house overlooked a desolate harbour where, some months previously, a small mountain of cement bags, most of which had now burst open, had been dumped with the intention of enlarging the harbour.

The days were unbelievably hot and humid and all we could do was to lie, stripped, on camp beds waiting for evening when the temperature would drop to about 100 degrees Fahrenheit. Our room faced the harbour where glassless windows overlooked the rotting bags of cement. Before midday each day a hot, on-shore breeze would pick up gradually covering our sweat-soaked bodies with powdered cement. When we were coated grey and the cement began to harden, we would leap up, throw buckets of tepid water over ourselves then return to our camp beds where the torment would start again.

In the evening, the governor of the province would send over a huge brass tray full of stewed sheep, camel and rice, tinned cheese, bread and jam and Coca-Cola. It all seemed a long way from the terrace of the St. Georges.

Finally, our escort of smiling, rascally-looking Yemenis arrived with bandoliers of cartridges across their chests and curved Yemeni daggers (*jambiahs*) strapped against their stomachs. They had no pockets in their robes, so their *jambiahs* were used, apart from killing people, to secure their personal effects. These usually included Marlboro cigarettes, matches, sometimes pens and paper, and packets of *qat*, a mild narcotic, which would all be stuffed in behind their daggers.

We were delighted to see them, and set out across the desert in an open truck which bounced past straw-roofed huts and negroid-looking inhabitants. Gradually, as we crossed the frontier and climbed, all this changed. Up in the mountains we passed villages with tall stone houses, each built like a small fortress from which, for centuries, the locals had conducted their tribal feuds.

As we progressed, other vehicles joined us on the first stage of our

1. R.B.'s morning shower outside village house, Cyprus, 1953.

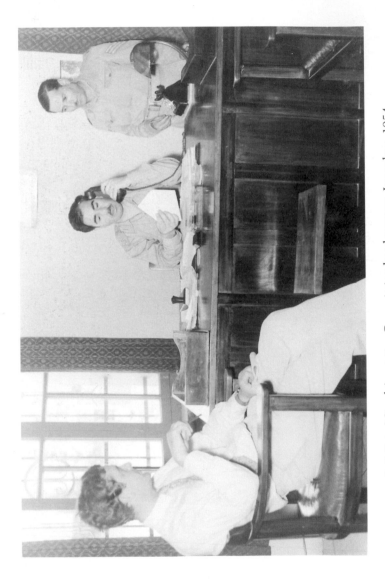

2. R.B. in Mixed Armistice Commission headquarters, Jerusalem, 1954.

3. King Hussein of Jordan with Lieutenant General John Glubb, visiting Jordan–Israel frontier villages, 1955. *Associated Press.*

4. US Marines landing in Lebanon, July 1958.

5. H.A.R. (Kim) Philby on family picnic in Lebanon.
Daughter Jennifer Beeston on donkey, 1958.

6. Kim Philby with Moyra and Jennifer & friends at picnic, 1958.

7. Ill-fated *Times* correspondent, David Holden with Egyptian
journalist Hariya Khairy, Cairo, 1958.

8. R.B.'s taxi stuck in sand in Syrian desert on way to cover Iraq revolution, July 1958.

9. Muslim rebels in Tripoli, Lebanon, 1958.

10. Soviet Embassy diplomats in Amman, Jordan, 1966. KGB 'bait' for King Hussein, Olga Petrovsky (second from right) is standing next to her KGB agent 'husband'.

11. Yemen's exiled Imam al Badr (left) emerging from his cave in Northern Yemen with royalist tribesmen, 1963.

12. The Imam's headquarters, Northern Yemen, 1963.

13. A tribesman holding remains of an Egyptian poison-gas bomb, Al Kawma, Northern Yemen, 1963.

14. Al Kawma village in a then unmapped part of Northern Yemen, 1963.

15. Civil disturbances in Aden, 1966.

16. R.B.'s son in Mombasa with Kenyan nanny Esther, 1964.

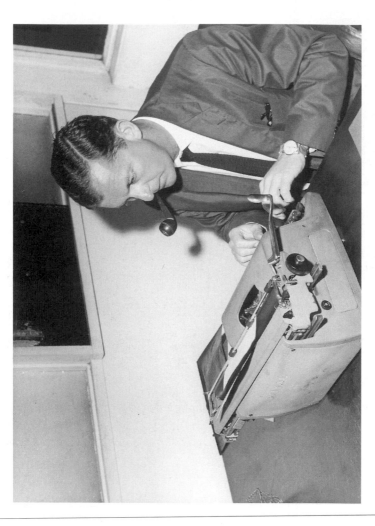

17. R.B. in *East African Standard* office, Nairobi, on day of his expulsion from Kenya, December 1964.

18. R.B. arriving at Heathrow airport after his expulsion
from Kenya, December 1964.

19. R.B. covering Senate Watergate hearings,
Washington, 1974.

20. R.B. covering October Revolution day parade,
Red square, Moscow, 1977.

21. Moyra and son Richard, Moscow 1996.

22. R.B. in London, December 1996.

Ким
Филби

МОЯ
ТАЙНАЯ
ВОЙНА

**ВОСПОМИНАНИЯ
СОВЕТСКОГО
РАЗВЕДЧИКА**

*Перевод с английского
П. Н. Видуэцкого
и С. К. Рощина*

To Moyra and Dick,

From Russia with Love,

Kimanina

25. X. 82

Ордена Трудового
Красного Знамени
Военное
издательство
Министерства
обороны СССР
Москва — 1982

23. The Russian version of Kim Philby's book,
My Secret War, with inscription.

journey to the Imam's base camp at Washa, commanded by Prince Abdul Rahman, the Imam's uncle. The most eminent personage in our convoy was the Naib of Ibb, a stubborn old white-bearded religious leader who showed a total lack of concern for safety – his or ours. He set the pace for our journey, insisting on five long prayer sessions a day. The Egyptian Air Force was active in the area and the Naib would unhesitatingly choose the most exposed piece of terrain to lay down his mat and face Mecca. None of our pleadings could persuade him to cut short his prayers, but Allah appeared to be on his side and we were never spotted. After dark, towards the end of our journey, however, we came under fire from Egyptian machine-guns and mortars, and had to complete our journey without lights.

From the base camp, we set off on foot across the mountains for an all-night climb to the Imam's headquarters at Al Qara. For our two guides, the journey must have been the equivalent of a walk down the road to the pub. They took nothing with them, ate our sandwiches and drank all our water. Just before dawn, exhausted by the climb and with a terrible thirst we found a filthy pool inches thick in green slime. We had to force our water bottles through it to get to the water below, which we drank, and which did us no harm.

An hour or so later we reached our destination – a rugged mountain area with a Yemeni tribesman sitting on every rock ready to take on the Egyptian air force with his old Italian musket or his British Enfield 303. A train of camels loaded with boxes of ammunition had just arrived and was being unloaded. But outside the Imam's residence, a cave, four feet high and protected by a rough wall across the mouth against Egyptian air attacks, all was quiet. The Imam, we learned, as a result of too much whisky and *qat* was sleeping off a hangover. He emerged about midday, not looking too good, and began meeting delegations of tribal sheikhs who were in the market for free rifles.

The Imam's addiction to *qat*, an unattractive habit, was shared by most Yemenis. The green sprigs look and taste like a privet hedge and take a lot of chewing to get results. By that time the chewer has a huge wad of leaves puffing out his cheek, giving the impression of mumps or bad toothache, and his mouth is stained a bright green. Tribal warfare between the Yemenis usually ceases in the afternoon when by mutual consent everything stops for *qat*.

It was during our visit to Al Qara that we first heard reports, that we were unable to confirm, of Egyptian gas attacks on Yemeni villages. After talking to the Imam and some of his commanders we decided to return to Saudi Arabia to file our stories and made a fearful night-time descent down the mountain perched on two of the Imam's friskiest mules. On our return to Jizan we found that it had just been subjected to two days of bombing by the Egyptian Air Force, and most of its population had fled and were living on beaches on nearby islands in the Red Sea.

Poison Gas

The Yemeni war had attracted a number of British soldiers of fortune. Among the jolliest I met on my journey were the two soldiers of fortune, Colonels Neil (Billy) McLean, then MP for Inverness, and David Smiley. They were old comrades from the Second World War, had fought together in the Balkans with the SOE (Special Operations Executive), had never quite grown up, and enjoyed a good fight. They were having a great time in the mountains advising the royalist forces on tactics and weapons, with all expenses paid by the Saudi government, and could think of nowhere they would rather be – except perhaps in their respective castles in Spain.

McLean had the ear of Harold Macmillan and helped persuade him to wage a very effective clandestine war against President Nasser in Northern Yemen, dropping thousands of rifles by air to the tribesmen and sending in other military supplies by camel from Aden and Saudi Arabia. McLean and Smiley were joined for a time by the explorer Wilfred Thesiger who shared a trench with them during an Egyptian Air Force bombing attack, and Colonel David Stirling, the founder of the SAS, set up an office in London to recruit mercenaries to fight in northern Yemen.

Much to their surprise, I did not share the enthusiasm of McLean and Smiley for life in the Yemen, and after the discomforts and uncertainties of the place was only too pleased to return to London. But only a fortnight later I found myself back in that depressing Jizan guest-house, and this time alone.

I had thought that I had seen the last of Yemen but in London found my Managing Editor, Pop Pawley, much excited by my reports of the poison gas attacks. They had also aroused the interest of the Foreign Office who had been on to Pawley about my report. They were pursuing the alarming theory that the Soviet Union, with close links with the Egyptians in those days, might be using the Egyptian Air Force to conduct experiments on Yemeni royalists with secret new nerve gas weapons.

Pawley asked me to go straight back to Yemen and try to reach the mountain village of Al Kawma where I had heard there had been a gas attack. The *Telegraph* arranged for me to see a Foreign Office gas warfare expert who lent me a gas mask, although he was not very reassuring, saying that if it was nerve gas that the Egyptians were using the mask would be of no use anyway. I then went to my surprised local chemist in Barnes and purchased some thick rubber gloves, tongs, specimen jars, and water purifying tablets for the journey.

When I arrived back in Jizan, I found myself something of a local hero. The governor of the province had been reluctant to be the conveyor of bad news and the Saudi government was totally unaware of the extent of the Egyptian bombing raids on the south of the Kingdom until my reports of the attacks had been translated and broadcast in the BBC Arabic service. Since then, emergency assistance had been sent to Jizan by the Saudi ruler King Feisal.

Escorted by another set of Yemeni royalist tribesmen I reached Al Kawma village late one night after a three-day journey. I knew we had come to the right place when, hundreds of yards away across the valley, I could hear the pitiful coughing of the gassed villagers which continued throughout the night. About a third of the hundred or so villagers had been gassed, seven had died. The face of one woman had turned a vivid yellow and another had been blinded. One little boy, Mohammed Nasser aged about 12, had a perpetual cough and deep blister wounds on his body.

As a result of my report he was brought back to Britain and treated for the effects of what was apparently mustard gas. I collected the bomb, shaped like a wheel with 15 canisters about the size of a carburettor, put it on a mule and took it back to Jeddah. From there it was sent to the United Nations, provoking a long controversy over what chemicals had been used in the bomb since it had been exposed for several weeks to sun and rain.

Meanwhile, the Egyptians, whose troops proved totally unfit for mountain warfare, failed to conquer the north but kept up their poison gas attacks with increasing intensity in an effort to cower the royalist tribes. The International Red Cross, which sent in units to Yemeni villages to aid the victims, knew perfectly well that poison gas was being used, but were unwilling to say so publicly for fear of compromising their neutrality. Finally, however, an IRC convoy on its way to a village stricken by a gas attack was bombed by Egyptian aircraft. This proved to be the last straw. The Red Cross came out with a public statement and Egypt was at last condemned by the UN for using chemical warfare against civilian populations.

The publication of the Red Cross report came just before the outbreak of the June 1967 Arab–Israeli Six Days' War. Following Egypt's humiliating defeat, President Nasser lost his appetite for the war in

Yemen and withdrew the Egyptian expeditionary force supporting the republicans.

The removal of the Egyptian presence from south Arabia should have relieved the pressure on the British in Aden, but by that time it was too late and Britain's allies in Aden, the sheikhs and sultans of the interior, were thoroughly demoralised. The extent of anti-British feeling in south Arabia during the Arab–Israeli war, and the failure of attempts to build a broadly based government, all contributed to an air of despondency among British officials when I returned there in June 1967.

I had been covering the Aden story fairly frequently, ever since 1958. At first you could swim from the beaches, visit the emirates in the mountainous interior, even dine off gold plate with Tony Besse, the richest trader in the Colony, but each time I returned the perimeter of safety had contracted and the terrorists' grip had tightened. Apart from a series of bomb attacks, by 1967 Britons, both military and civilian, were being shot in the street and even a brief visit to the shops was an uneasy experience.

In 1963 Britain had created a Federation of Emirates but this had only increased the opposition of the Aden townspeople who feared domination by the tribal states. The last British hope was the South Arabian Army, but this became infiltrated by nationalist forces and weakened by tribal divisions.

Any prospect of trust and co-operation between the federal army and British forces in Aden was destroyed on 20 June 1967. Twenty-two British soldiers, including Royal Northumberland Fusiliers and some Argyll and Sutherland Highlanders, were killed and others were held hostage. We piled into taxis from the Crescent Hotel to take us to the military police barracks where the mutiny had broken out, but came under fire from mutineers and had to withdraw.

The Crater district of Aden, a stronghold of anti-British feeling, was in the hands of the mutineers. Lieutenant Colonel Colin Mitchell, or 'Mad Mitch' as he became known for his Aden exploits, had just arrived in Aden to command the Argylls. He urged an occupation of Crater but this was refused by the GOC Middle East Land Forces Major General Philip Tower. Then against orders and before dawn, Mitchell marched his Highlanders into Crater and the startled inhabitants woke up to the sound of the bagpipes. I arrived there with Joe Morris to find all roads out of Crater manned by troops with fixed bayonets and soldiers on the rooftops of the highest buildings. Mitchell, a tough, no-nonsense soldier with a bit of a showman about him, was touring the town in a Land Rover. He was behaving more like a mayor than the commander of an occupation force, asking the locals about their problems, and, amazingly for that sullen town, was being received with broad smiles.

In his battalion headquarters he gave us a briefing on his methods of controlling the town. Then he took us up to the top floor of a building occupied by the Highlanders. 'Look through that,' he said, pointing to a telescopic rifle on a fixed mounting. Its target was the entrance to a local mosque. In the past, terrorists in Crater after an attack had made a habit of disappearing into the nearest mosque. Now every mosque in town had a sniper's rifle pointing at it.

'Mad Mitch' became an instant hero among the British public tired of reading stories about the success of anti-British terrorists in Aden. Mitchell held Crater successfully until the British withdrawal in November. However, the army never forgave his success and he was passed over for promotion and resigned.

During 1967 a totally new force appeared on the Aden scene – the National Liberation Front (NLF). Previously, the only nationalist organisation had been the Egyptian-backed Front for the Liberation of South Yemen (FLOSY). No one seemed to know where the NLF had come from, but they were tough Marxists who began a brutal war of elimination against the pro-Egyptian FLOSY supporters who were forced to flee into Yemen.

It was the NLF who took over control when Britain finally gave up its efforts to sustain the South Arabian Federation, and the British presence was soon replaced by the East Germans and Czechs of the Soviet bloc.

6

East Africa

The Doomed Sultan

Flanked by two tall, cynical, men-of-the-world, Prince Philip and the Colonial and Commonwealth Secretary Duncan Sandys, the some-what effeminate Sultan of Zanzibar, all dressed up for independence, looked lonely and exceedingly vulnerable. 'How long before we'll hear firing outside the palace?' I remember whispering to the *Daily Express* correspondent. A Royal Marine band was playing the national anthem at around midnight on 9 December 1963 as the Union Jack was lowered for the last time over Zanzibar.

That date, when Zanzibar became an independent state inside the Commonwealth, was to signal the final eclipse of a thousand years of Arab power in East Africa, abandoning Sultan Seyyid Jamshid bin Abdullah to the protection of a few dozen doubtfully loyal policemen and the best-of-luck wishes of Prime Minister Sir Alec Douglas-Home.

In their prime, the Omani and Hadramaut Arabs in Zanzibar had for centuries dominated all East Africa, plundering slaves from deep in the interior and also piling up fortunes from trade in ivory and spices. 'When the pipes play in Zanzibar', went the African saying 'all Africa dances'. Tens of thousands of Africans every year had passed through Zanzibar's slave market for export, but some had remained to cultivate the island's clove plantations. Descendants of these slaves were now in no mood to continue to live under an Arab aristocracy – a small minority of the population, emasculated by a century of benign British protection.

After three years of working out of Fleet Street, I had just been appointed *The Daily Telegraph*'s East African correspondent, based in Nairobi, at a time when *Uhuru* – Freedom – was much in the air. Uganda and Tanganyika had just received their independence, with

Kenya, the most sophisticated of the East African states, and Zanzibar waiting in the wings.

British official opinion had been scornful of the mess the Belgians had made in the Congo and were determined that British East Africa would not go the same way. It very nearly did when Zanzibar set off a chain reaction throughout the region. And eventually, only a decade or so later, the horrors of the Congo were more than duplicated in Uganda, while the eccentric, ideological socialist policies of President Julius Nyerere transformed Tanzania into one of the poorest nations in the world.

I had flown to Zanzibar to cover independence. It had the atmosphere of a friendly tropical island that had been snoring away for generations – a little-changed Victorian colonial backwater, with its narrow lanes and mosques and smells of spices. I put up at the English Club, a faded nineteenth century relic guarded by two brass cannons. Inside were overhead fans, a library of books mostly on hunting, shooting and fishing, a bar and a billiards room. The rules of a Victorian gentlemen's club were still applied with vigour by the English Secretary, and, despite the tropics, guests were required to dress for dinner.

Looking back, it seems strange that Britain should have gone to so much trouble to put on such a show – the Duke of Edinburgh, the Commonwealth Minister, the *Ark Royal* with its band and honour guard – and then just to fly off and leave the Sultan and his island, the newest member of the Commonwealth, so unprotected against the winds of change in Africa. Certainly the omens were there to be seen. In the Arab parts of Zanzibar there were flags and bunting and smiling faces, but the African quarters were sullen and silent on independence day as we all took off for the next event – Kenya's independence ceremony only two days later.

Revolution

Kenya's independence went off quietly and smoothly with its new head of state, Jomo Kenyatta, once the bogeyman of the white settlers, now miraculously transformed into the *Mzee*, the wise old man and father of the nation and protector of the whites. In Zanzibar, however, the government and sultanate was swept away just a month later, on 11 January 1964, when about 20 African rebels, led by an unhinged soldier of fortune and self-styled Field Marshal, John Okello, a young Ugandan trained in Cuba, stormed the Zanzibar police barracks and distributed weapons to the African population.

It was all over by dawn. In the following days, thousands of Arabs and Indians were slaughtered, their bodies littering the Zanzibar beaches, while the surviving Arab population was shipped back to Arabia.

Despite warnings by Zanzibar Radio that unauthorised visitors would be shot, there was a scramble by the press to get in. Most chose to cross from the East African mainland by *dhow*. But I joined forces with *The Sunday Times* correspondent Richard Cox, a cool, reserved Englishman and a bit of a loner, who was a trained pilot and a Territorial Army paratrooper. He was just the man for the story, although he did make me rather uneasy by flying the plane in his carpet slippers.

We chartered a tiny two seater from Nairobi Airport, put down in Dar-es-Salaam for fuel and then set out uneasily across the Indian Ocean for Zanzibar. The neat and tidy airport I had left only a month ago was unrecognisable. The control tower and airport offices had been smashed, the shops looted, and broken glass and rubble lay everywhere.

The airport was still officially closed and when we landed we were immediately surrounded by a mob of excited, half-naked Zanzibaris armed with clubs, cutlasses and knives who led us off under detention. Somehow, we managed to persuade them to put a call through to the Revolutionary Headquarters and contacted the newly appointed Defence Minister, Mohammed Babu, who eventually turned up with his own armed bodyguard and freed us. Babu, rather a jolly man from one of the old Zanzibar opposition parties, drove us into town in a car packed with his guards.

We turned up at the Club where the desperate English Secretary, the stickler for correct dress and club rules, was nervously serving meals to a bunch of cut-throats mostly favouring Cuban revolutionary-style dress with bandoliers, wide-brim straw hats and machetes.

Peter Younghusband and his *Daily Express* colleague John Monks went to Zanzibar by *dhow*. Before the revolution, Younghusband had been enjoying a series of scoops and Monks had received a rather ignominious cable from the *Express* telling him not to let Peter out of his sight. John, unfortunately, was very pale skinned and during the crossing to Zanzibar in an open *dhow* became terribly sunburned. Arriving in the evening just outside the harbour, Peter, at the risk of being shot, dived overboard and swam to shore to get medical help for his colleague.

Climbing onto the harbour he found himself looking into the barrel of a sten gun and was marched off to the police station. He was briefly locked away in a room where he spotted a telephone, picked it up and dictated his story to his stringer in Dar-es-Salaam. 'I swam ashore tonight . . .' Poor John Monks was scooped again!

A group of British and American correspondents who came in in another *dhow* were given a rough time. The presence of the Americans convinced the revolutionaries that they were all working for the CIA and at one stage they were marched off into a cemetery where they fully expected to be shot. Richard and I received better treatment and were taken off to interview the Field Marshal. We drove past the stadium where hundreds of Arabs had been rounded up, but had no idea at that time of the slaughter that was going on throughout the island.

Okello's office in the police headquarters was guarded by a huge, ferocious-looking black woman armed with a long, old-fashioned British bayonet. At his desk, dressed like a Cuba revolutionary, sat Okello. Lying stretched out, flat on the floor in front of him, as we entered was a comrade pointing a Bren machine-gun at us. The Field Marshal, wild-eyed and fairly mad, ranted on about ending centuries of Arab slavery. However, despite the Bren gun, I would have said he was really no more intimidating than Margaret Thatcher with a glint in her eye at some of her press conferences I have attended.

At the start of the coup, Okello and his thugs could have been put down by a platoon of British troops. The newly appointed British High Commissioner TH Crosthwaite had the authority to call in a British warship – two of which were in the area – but decided not to do so, and instead advised British residents, when encountering any problems, to smile and give the 'V' sign – a symbol adopted by the revolutionaries. He certainly did not earn much respect from the British community and after meeting him one of the American correspondents remarked to me 'he's not the sort of British diplomat we were taught about in high school'. Britain, however, was no doubt anxious not to be seen propping up by armed force a minority Arab government in East Africa at a time of volatile African nationalism throughout the continent. So thousands of Arabs had to die while the Sultan finished up living on a small pension in Southsea.

Richard Cox and I, meanwhile, had to get out to file our story and managed to persuade the revolutionary authorities to give us an exit permit. We returned to the chaos of the airport where an embryo emigration control had been set up by revolutionaries barely able to read or write. 'Who are the two correspondents?' the controller asked. We pointed to each other and he looked suspiciously at our passports. 'Where is the pilot?' I pointed to Richard. 'No he is the correspondent, where is the pilot of your plane?' 'He is the correspondent and the pilot,' I replied. 'No, no, no, if he is the correspondent, where is the pilot?'

This went on for some time until, in exasperation, he waved us through. Our little plane was where we had left it on the runway. We climbed aboard, but as Richard was about to check it out suddenly the airport staff and a bunch of shouting Africans waving machetes and guns started rushing down the runway towards us. The engine roared and Richard was away in a flash as we heard shots being fired at our plane. I looked back to see the angry little group on the runway, and wondered if Richard had had time to check to see if we had enough petrol to get us back across the Indian Ocean.

A House-Warming

The day after my return from Zanzibar we gave our house-warming party. Moyra had arrived in Nairobi a few days earlier with our two daughters and our ten-month-old baby, Richard. We had just moved into a large house outside Nairobi with a wild garden which led down to a stream where a leopard lived. I inherited the home security system, a Kenyan dressed in an old army great coat, armed with an *assegai*, who used to rise up terrifyingly from the bushes to confront us with his spear when we returned at night from late parties.

About 20 people, mainly press, arrived for the house- warming, but when Moyra returned from the kitchen after preparing some food the room was almost deserted. We had just had news of an army mutiny in Tanganyika and most of the guests had rushed off to file their stories. British officers from the Tanganyika rifles had been put under house arrest by the mutineers, President Julius Nyerere had uncourageously disappeared into hiding and the mobs were out looting hotels and shops.

I arrived in Dar-es-Salaam just as British commandos were storming ashore and the mutineers were fleeing into the bush. Within two days army mutinies erupted in both Uganda and Kenya. With the example of Zanzibar in mind, this time British forces were sent in immediately. Within days they had restored order in all three territories, saving East Africa from what would have certainly been a repetition of the Congo.

But the events illustrated what a fragile framework Britain was leaving behind after half a century in East Africa. And everyone's worst fears were realised a decade later when hundreds of thousands

perished during the bloody regime of that British army-trained product – the good soldier Idi Amin.

After this hectic start, we began to settle into the life of a newly
independent African state which, outwardly, looked little changed
from its colonial days. The beautiful, equatorial highlands of Kenya
were undiscovered by the West until European explorers reached
them in the nineteenth century. The region was thinly populated and
so primitive that in the more remote areas even the wheel was
unknown before the arrival of the Europeans.

Britain first gained concessionary rights to Mombasa and the coastline from the Sultan of Zanzibar in 1887 and the British and German
governments divided up East Africa at about that time. Kenya went to
Britain and Tanganyika to Germany. The Kenyan highlands were
first opened up to White settlement at the end of the century when
Indian labour was brought in to build a railroad from Mombasa,
through the highlands to Lake Victoria. Thousands of workers died,
many taken by lions, in building the railway. Nairobi was just a rail-
head camp in Masai territory, 5,500 feet up, but became the capital of
Kenya Colony and centre of the prosperous, European-dominated
highlands farming area.

After the Second World War more British and South African set-
tlers poured into the colony. Growing tensions over land led to the
Mau-Mau rebellion among the Kikuyu people, the arrest of the
Kikuyu leader Jomo Kenyatta and eventually independence under
Kenyatta's leadership.

Kenyatta, described by a former British governor of Kenya as 'a
leader into darkness and to death' appeared to bear no grudge
against the whites for his long incarceration. A thoroughly pragmatic
man, he realised that the security of the state depended on British
army officers and police and the knowledge that British troops could
be brought in at short notice. Indeed, his personal bodyguard and
close friend was a senior British police officer. At the same time, he
had to play to the crowd and did nothing to stop the deportation by
his Interior Minister Oginga Odinga of a stream of Britons, including
press and members of the security forces who had played a key role
in suppressing the Mau-Mau insurgency.

The Mau-Mau emergency had ended a few years earlier after the
deaths of about 13,000 blacks and 32 whites. I was surprised on arrival
to learn of the small death toll of white settlers, after so much publicity. It was in fact a good deal lower than the number of Britons
killed by *EOKA* while I was in Cyprus. However, the obscenities of the
Mau-Mau oath-taking ceremonies and the killing of isolated farmers

and their families by their terrorised servants had a nightmarish quality which still left a chill and sense of threat about a highland Kenyan
farm.

Hundreds of Mau-Mau fighters had chosen to remain in the forests
of Mount Kenya long after the uprising had been crushed. Soon
after independence, Jomo Kenyatta summoned them out. I was in
Nairobi at the time and the sight of the so-called 'forest fighters',
dressed in filthy monkey skins and with their matted hair hanging
down below their shoulders, swaggering through the streets of
Nairobi, not surprisingly caused some alarm among the whites.

At Nyeri stadium in the central highlands I attended a ceremony
where 1,500 Mau-Mau pledged allegiance to the new flag, but they
expected to play a hero's role in the new state. However, they were
yesterday's men – and many soon finished up in gaol.

Today's men were the Kikuyu political leaders busily engaged in
taking over from the white Bwanas, moving into their farms, busi-
nesses and clubs, seizing their directorships while creating a
Kikuyu-dominated one-party state. At the Nairobi or Lumuru races
you would see the Kikuyu racehorse owners dressed in well-cut
English tweeds happily taking up the white man's burden.

They were the dominant tribe. The second largest was the Luo.
And the only person the young Kikuyu leaders really feared was the
Luo leader Tom Mboya, who was far too smart for their liking. So
eventually, with a nod from Kenyatta, they killed him.

Happy Valley

Kenya's white society was quite neatly divided between the two main
clubs in the capital – the Nairobi Club and the Muthaiga Country
Club. The Nairobi was the respectable, boring one. Members were
mainly bankers, businessmen and civil servants whose roots were not
in East Africa. The Muthaiga was thoroughly unreconstructed – a
throwback to the pioneering colonial days earlier in the century,
whose members, mostly farmers now of a certain age, still came in
from the country for a little hell-raising.

On the eve of independence, the club committee had an emergency meeting to decide whether they should change the rules and
allow black membership. After much heart-searching they decided to
do so, only to find there was no rule which excluded a black joining.
The Muthaiga had never even remotely considered the possibility of
a black member!

The boisterous atmosphere of a weekend party at the Muthaiga was like that of an army mess, although most of the members were far too old for active service. In the Muthaiga the spirit of the Happy Valley ('are you married or do you live in Kenya?') set still flickered. And there were still people in the Club who claimed to know the truth about Kenya's most famous murder mystery – the shooting of Lord Errol, whose affair with the future Lady Delamere blossomed at the Muthaiga.

Following a rowdy evening, often involving games which combined a version of rugger and musical chairs, watched impassively by the black servants, the bills would be handed out to members for damage to club property. But standards had to be kept up. On one occasion when I was there an angry farmer's wife reported the barman for addressing her in English instead of Swahili. Most of the members spoke some Swahili, the pronunciation of which was made rather hilarious by their exaggerated upper-class English accents.

During this time, Celia Sandys, the young, attractive daughter of the then Commonwealth Secretary, lived in Kenya, fitting effortlessly into the fading Happy Valley society. One day she strode into the Muthaiga men's bar and ordered a drink. The male members deeply offended, walked out, and one was heard to mutter 'I always knew there was bad blood in that family'.

Kenya has always had a rather *louche* reputation – 'a place in the sun for shady people'– partly no doubt out of envy for people living 6,000 feet up on the Equator who seemed to be having far too good a time. But although many of the white farmers played hard and drank hard, they were also incredibly tough and resilient. They had carved out their farms from an inhospitable and dangerous environment, subject to devastating droughts and unknown diseases that wiped out cattle and crops. Usually with slender financial resources, they had built up dairy, cattle and coffee industries which were the backbone of the country's economy.

Their houses were modest, homemade, with a corrugated iron roof, verandas, a big fireplace, some silver and a few good pieces of furniture. They would think nothing of driving 60 miles on a slippery *muram* track for a drinks party, or to stitch up a farmhand mauled by a leopard.

We arrived for a weekend with farming friends, Dick and Claudia Slaughter, to learn that their next-door neighbour, a few miles down the track, had just been trampled into his lawn by an elephant which had strayed onto his land. Claudia kept horses and Dick was employed by the Kenya Land Settlement and Development Board which played a vital role in Kenya's transition to independence.

Huge areas of rich farmland in the White Highlands had to be taken over to satisfy the land hunger of the Kikuyu – who had one of the world's highest birthrates – or risk revolution. The white farmers had to be compensated. From a modest sum provided by the British government, the Board compensated the whites and provided development funds for blacks in a scheme which proved remarkably successful. Although many of the white farmers emigrated to Rhodesia or South Africa, some stayed behind to work as farm managers for Kikuyu owners on some of the larger estates. Politically, the scheme was a success but it devastated a large proportion of Kenya's agricultural sector which had provided a highly successful export industry.

I visited one large farm in the White Highlands only days after it had been handed over to dozens of Kikuyu families. Already the rolling pastures, which had looked like Wiltshire farmland, were being chopped up into plots where maize was being planted to provide a bare subsistence for the new owners.

Expelled

I had a desk in Nairobi at the *East African Standard*, a paper that for years had been the right-wing voice of the settlers but was quickly adjusting to the new regime. Shortly after my arrival my Foreign Editor, Ricky Marsh, paid a visit and together we went to see Oginga Odinga who was involved in a power struggle with Kenyatta.

Odinga, who had a vested interest in worsening relations with the West, was thoroughly hostile and blasted off against the British press, and in particular *The Daily Telegraph*. He seemed slightly deranged and left us in no doubt that he would be delighted to get rid of me and the *Telegraph* bureau. He was later gaoled, but meanwhile Kenyatta, determined to give Odinga enough rope to hang himself, did nothing to interfere with the stream of expulsions of Westerners ordered by Odinga, which created an atmosphere of fear and deteriorating morale among the foreign community. The American Embassy took a robust stand against all this, protesting against expulsions of Americans and the anti-Western, pro-communist attitude of Odinga and his followers.

The British High Commission adopted a weak and placatory line and did little to stand up for the rights of British citizens in Kenya. Meanwhile, the carefully laid plans of Britain for democracy and regional co-operation were being ditched. Kenya, which began independence with a thoroughly alien Westminster parliamentary system, was heading for a one-party state while the East African Federation of Kenya, Uganda and Tanzania, so carefully nurtured by Britain, began to fall apart.

The *East African Standard* started imposing its own self-censorship on stories in any way critical of newly independent Kenya. Reuters, involved in a big sales drive throughout Africa, also became compromised. It persuaded the *Standard* to relinquish its representation of Reuters in Kenya and handed it over to the newly formed government-controlled Kenya News Agency (KNA).

Under the deal, the Reuters' file was transmitted to the KNA which would then distribute it to East African Kenya newspapers and radio stations under Reuters' name. As the new service started up, I obtained a copy of instructions issued to KNA editors about how to process incoming copy from Reuters before distribution – for example, any reference in Reuters to Southern Rhodesia or its Prime Minister had always to be prefaced with the words 'white racist'. Any story critical of Kenya had to be referred to the chief editor, who normally killed it.

I had the entire memo published in *The Daily Telegraph* the day before a Reuters director, Patrick Crosse, arrived in Nairobi to celebrate the deal. We had been invited to a dinner to meet Cross, but after the publication of the memo our invitation was promptly cancelled. After the dinner an indignant Associate Press correspondent, Denis Neeld, told me that Crosse, mistaking him for me, had threatened to punch him in the nose.

In early December 1964, while I was covering a story in Ethiopia, *The Sunday Telegraph* sent a colleague, Douglas Brown, to do a piece on Kenya. A mutual friend of ours, Nancy Hoare, who worked for government protocol, tipped Brown off that Odinga was receiving secret shipments of small arms from China through Nairobi airport and was concealing them in the basement of the Ministry of the Interior.

The day after *The Sunday Telegraph* published the story, I was reading the wires in the *East African Standard* and saw a Kenya News Agency report that the Kenya government had declared Douglas Brown and myself prohibited immigrants and given me 24 hours to leave the country.

Pack and Follow

A rather embarrassed British official in the Kenya immigration department, a Colonel Mitchell came round to serve the expulsion order. When I pointed out that under the law I could appeal against the order, he said that I had already been booked on the BOAC flight to London the following evening and that was that.

The British Acting High Commissioner to whom I complained next morning failed to persuade Odinga to withdraw the expulsion order or even to extend the 24-hour period I had been given to leave the country. I then went to Government House where Malcolm MacDonald was living in great style with his Asian mistress, fulfilling the temporary role of Governor General before Kenyatta moved in. He listened to my case and then explained, in a memorable response, 'I would like to help you Beeston, but you see, in Kenya, I am in effect the Queen.'

The High Commission clearly wanted me to leave with the minimum of trouble or embarrassment. The Public Affairs Officer at the American Embassy, John Hogan, a friend of ours, hastily arranged a farewell party for me. It was attended by the American ambassador, while all the members of the British High Commission kept their heads down.

The party spilled over to the Nairobi airport bar where Moyra and the children and a number of colleagues came to see me off. But when I went to the ticket counter to purchase my ticket I became involved in a 'Catch-22' situation which kept the BOAC VC-10 waiting for over an hour.

At the counter, the airline agents handed me an air ticket paid for by the Kenyan government. I told them that I wished to buy my own ticket and could not accept free travel from the Kenyans. The airline agents said they could not sell me a ticket without an income tax clearance certificate which would take some days to obtain. I insisted that if I could not pay for my own ticket, I would not get on the plane, and returned to the party. Meanwhile, the Kenyan authorities told BOAC that the airliner could not leave without me.

Finally, Mitchell was summoned from Nairobi and ordered me to leave. When I refused he formally placed me under arrest and then escorted me to the aircraft. The situation by then had been explained to the long-suffering 110 passengers stuck on the runway. When I boarded they gave me a cheer, which I felt was far more than I deserved for the inconvenience I had caused them.

Moyra had to stay behind in Nairobi to pay for, pack and arrange the move back to London. In the midst of packing up Fiona, aged eight, had to have an operation for appendicitis which delayed the family's departure beyond Christmas. In the weeks before leaving, the British High Commission cut off all contact. None of our Commission friends or acquaintances called or even phoned. 'It was just like being sent to Coventry,' Moyra said. 'I ran into one High Commission wife while doing some shopping for Christmas and mentioned that things were difficult. 'I am really not surprised' she replied and scurried off. Thank God for our American and up-country farming friends who rallied round.'

Back in London, the *Telegraph* agreed to pay for rented accommodation for the family until I could be reassigned. I went round to a Kensington estate agent and rather grandly rented a house on the corner of Hyde Park Gate overlooking Kensington Gardens.

I hired a nanny for our temporary stay but was unable to contact her to postpone her arrival because of the delay over Fiona's appendix. She arrived one Sunday morning, looking gorgeous. When I suggested she come back later she said she had nowhere else to stay – so she moved in. A week or so later as I was leaving for the office, she came downstairs looking rather pale. I asked her if she was unwell, and she suddenly collapsed in tears sobbing 'you must have guessed, I'm pregnant!'

I quickly sent a message to Moyra, saying 'come back soon, the nanny's pregnant!'. Moyra and the children joined me just after Christmas, but I felt some reluctance to divulge our rather exalted address to the *Telegraph*, whose senior staff were inclined to live rather more modestly. When the subject came up I used to mutter something about a small flat in Kensington. My cover was blown when, one wintry afternoon, I returned to find to my great surprise the house surrounded by dozens of photographers, home reporters and foreign correspondents, many of whom were friends

Sir Winston Churchill, who lived a few houses down the road, had begun to die. A death watch had been started and all the press had been driven back by the police from Churchill's house to our corner. They were by now four or five deep outside our house and, during the next few weeks, I was given an insight of what it is like to be on the wrong side of a press stakeout. I struggled through to the front door and went over to the window on the park where I could hear someone shouting my name. 'Dick, can you take hold of this?' shouted Terry Spencer, a *Time* and *Life* photographer with whom I had been on several stories in Africa. He then proceeded to pass me, over the heads of the press and through the drawing-room window, a huge tripod and a lot of other very heavy photographic equipment.

Terry then came into the house, and found that my son Richard's bedroom had a perfect view of Churchill's house. He promptly moved Richard out and set up a camera with telephoto lenses and a tripod at the window to await a shot of Winston's coffin when it finally emerged. The *Telegraph*, having discovered my secret, staffed the house all day long. I remember asking one *Telegraph* reporter, who had his feet up on my study desk and spent most of his time on the phone to Churchill's doctor, Lord Moran, how he liked my accommodation. Looking up rather mournfully at the surroundings, he shook his head and replied 'I think you've rather overdone it old man'.

He was right. As the weeks went by, we had an endless stream of friends and colleagues dropping in for drinks or coffee, so that we took to going out for most meals and slipping back late at night. Finally, I found it a relief to leave Hyde Park Gate, just days before Churchill's funeral, to cover the Queen's visit to Ethiopia.

7

Vietnam

No Light at the End of the Tunnel

Just a few months later I found myself, improbably, shopping for stolen American army equipment in a huge open-air market in Saigon. You needed camouflage combat fatigues, a water bottle, haversack and ammunition boots, before the US forces would take you into battle, and Saigon's thriving black market was there to provide.

After my abrupt departure from Nairobi, the *Telegraph* decided to send me back to Beirut to share the coverage of the Middle East with Eric Downton. But since things were unusually quiet there I left to do a stint in Vietnam, at a time that turned out to be a turning-point in the Vietnam War. It was 1965, and the first regular American troops assigned for offensive action – two battalions of US Marines – were landing in Da-Nang. In January, President Johnson had been faced with two choices – to negotiate his way out of Vietnam or to commit America's military power to force a change in communist bloc policy in the Far East.

The French had learned their lesson in Vietnam during the French Indochina War which led to France's devastating defeat at Dien Bien Phu in 1954. The armistice agreement left Vietnam divided between the Ho Chi Minh communist government in the North and the pro-Western government of President Ngo Dinh Diem in the South. The United States, which had funded the French in their war against the Vietnamese communists, then became increasingly involved in combating the communist threat to the South with military and economic aid to the corrupt and repressive Diem regime.

By 1961, the South Vietnamese Viet Cong, supported by the

North, controlled about half of South Vietnam. In that year President Eisenhower sent in the first US support troops, ostensibly as advisers, to Vietnam. Their numbers were substantially increased by President Kennedy who backed a coup which led to the overthrow and execution of President Diem.

Ill-advised by his defence secretary Robert McNamara, Johnson in 1965 chose the all-out military option and committed America to the most divisive war it had fought since the Civil War. Already, by the time I arrived in July, the consequences of his decision were becoming apparent as the war took on an alarming new pitch of intensity.

In that year, the American casualty list of killed in action shot up from the previous year's level of 146 to 1,275 as did the level of Viet Cong attacks, ambushes, sabotage and infiltration. American forces increased from 23,000 at the start of the year to 190,000. This was to set a pattern of rapid escalation in which finally over half a million American forces were involved – with an ultimate US death toll of 56,000.

Reinforcements included the US First Infantry Division and what was thought to be America's war-winner, the First Air Cavalry (Air Mobile) Division. US military thinkers had become foolishly convinced by the French belief that only the lack of helicopters had led to France's final defeat at Dien Bien Phu. The Americans were determined not to make the same mistake, but seriously overestimated the role that the helicopter would play in the Vietnam War.

The year marked the failure of four years of attempting to fight the war by proxy – by assigning American military advisers to Vietnamese army combat units. Now the huge American military machine began to take over, backed by the largest US military call-up since the Korean War.

The United States was tired of being kicked around. The bombing of North Vietnam had begun and Saigon, when I arrived, was in a frenzy of military activity with the US Army, the Marines, the US Special forces, the CIA and psychological warfare units all competing for a piece of the action. At the same time, large-scale US bombing of North Vietnam had begun.

However, despite the massive and growing American military presence, Saigon still seemed like a city under siege, with the US military headquarters, the Military Assistance Command, Vietnam (MACV), a heavily defended citadel. From the top floor dining room of the Caravelle Hotel, where the *Telegraph* had booked a room for the duration, you could watch the flash of gunfire and hear bombs and shells exploding in the surrounding jungle as the US military tried to seek out and destroy its invisible enemies.

Saigon was booming. Its streets were filled with motorised rickshaws, its innumerable bars and brothels were packed with American clients, while some delightful, small French restaurants still existed as a reminder of the days when Saigon was an elegant French Colonial town. The Cercle Royale continued to be the ultimate in Saigon society, frequented by wealthy French landowners, Vietnamese black marketeers, businessmen and generals, the patrician American Ambassador Henry Cabot Lodge and senior members of the US military.

Inside the American fortress headquarters, the MACV, I was introduced to the US Commander in Chief, General William Westmoreland. He was a handsome, confident, West Pointer who looked like a Hollywood hero but emerged as a very limited military strategist. With a formidable back-up of maps, statistics and aides he solemnly assured me, in the phrase that became the cliché of the war, that he could see 'the light at the end of the tunnel'. Later, the phrase became a mockery, but in those early days it seemed hard to imagine that such a formidable force as was being assembled by Westmoreland could not prevail.

However, suspicions were already growing that the MACV figures of the enemy 'body count' – the one measure used by the American military to calculate the success of the war – were being wildly exaggerated to persuade Congress that the war was being won. Estimates of enemy strength were equally fraudulent, deliberately playing down the size of the Viet Cong forces and the North Vietnamese regulars operating in the South, so as not to scare Capitol Hill.

President Lyndon Johnson did not want to hear any bad news. McNamara and his other close, pro-war advisers did their best to prevent it reaching him, and the warnings of the CIA, almost alone in its pessimism over the war, were ignored. Thus the stage was set for the whole Vietnam disaster – and the great anti-Vietnam war movement in America which brought about Johnson's downfall three years later.

A Dirty War

Among most Americans in Saigon, however, the spirit was gung-ho. Mr Gung-ho himself was Barry Zorthian, director of JUSPAO, the Joint US Public Affairs Office, who arranged correspondents' trips to the fighting. Barry, an irrepressible Armenian American who lived and breathed public relations was happily dropping millions of leaflets over Vietnam to win the hearts and minds of the nation and convince the natives of the inevitability of an American victory.

The press were pouring in to provide stories for the voracious TV networks, and even for obscure hometown papers of Middle America with local boys at the front. Apart from many veteran correspondents, such as the *New York Times*' Scotty Reston, who was given three-star general treatment by the military, scores of young reporters and photographers began their careers making their reputations working as stringers for wire services and networks covering the war.

Those were the days before demoralisation and drugs took over in the American forces and the military was looking good. But already America was getting its hands dirty, turning to more sinister methods to defeat the enemy. High-level, indiscriminate bombing of Vietnam had begun, the lethal, cancer-causing chemical 'Agent Orange' was being used to defoliate huge areas of forest, and villages were being destroyed by US shelling 'in order to save them'. Shocking images began appearing on American TV screens, such as the notorious occasion when US Marines set fire to a Vietnamese village with a Zippo lighter. American advisers were filmed standing by as their South Vietnam allies tortured and killed Viet Cong suspects, or as US planes napalmed Vietnamese villages.

One of my first combat stories was billed by JUSPAO as the largest joint US–South Vietnamese army operation against Vietcong forces. Dressed up as an unlikely looking GI, I was airlifted along with several colleagues to the battle zone, only a short flight from Saigon. When we were picked up, the sky was black with helicopters and it seemed almost inconceivable that any rag-tag army in black pyjamas could stand up to such formidable military might.

The operation was set out like a military exercise. US tanks and artillery were all lined up in a large clearing to give overhead support fire to a regiment of slight, boyish looking Vietnamese who were being sent into the forest to attack a suspected Viet Cong concentration which had already been attacked by B52 bombers.

I was standing next to an American tank commander, who was happily blasting away along with the artillery, when a frantic order came through to stop firing. The American shelling had fallen short onto their unfortunate Vietnamese allies. We waited in silence as eventually the 'friendly fire' casualties began appearing from the forest, pathetic, bloody and broken figures carried out by their stunned comrades.

That was it for the day. The helicopters returned to pick us up and that evening I was back at the Caravelle bar wondering whether the Americans really were getting their war right.

At about that time JUSPAO and some of the press corps were involved with the problem of a middle-aged colleague who was badly missing his wife, but was worried about the consequences of picking up an embarrassing disease from the local bar girls. Somehow, he involved us all in his concern until someone in the press office heard of an amateur, a pretty Vietnamese schoolgirl who could occasionally be persuaded to provide her services for a fee.

After days of planning, Frank's night of love was arranged at his room in the Caravelle. He was not to be disturbed and I was deputed to intercept his service messages and file any stories in his name. Next day at the press centre we all crowded round Frank expecting to see a new man. 'How did it go?' we asked. But Frank looked as disconsolate as ever. 'She stayed up late at night finishing off her homework,' he said sorrowfully. 'Then when she finally came to bed she said she was too tired and had a headache.'

The heaviest fighting that year was the struggle to control South Vietnam's central highlands. I covered a typical operation through a chance meeting with the American Chief of Operations, General Du Puy, who gave me a lift in his helicopter on a flight to reach a beleaguered special forces camp at Duc Co, close to the Cambodian border. American and Vietnamese forces had been under siege for five weeks and General Du Puy was bringing the defenders the good news that a relief column was fighting its way through.

Unfortunately, what the Saigon black market had failed to provide was a flack jacket, and as we boarded the helicopter I noticed that the general and his companions all wisely took theirs off and sat firmly on them. I clenched my knees and tried to make as small a target as I could for Viet Cong ground fire as we flew off in a scene that might have come straight from the film *Apocalypse Now*.

The military was clearly determined not to lose its chief of ops. To protect their man an army spotter plane flew ahead of us, pinpointing targets with smoke bombs while attack helicopters cut a fiery swathe through the jungle with rockets and machine-guns. At the same time, fighter bombers swept the area with bombs and napalm as we made our Wagnerian arrival at the special forces camp.

We may not have killed any Viet Cong, but we certainly beat hell out of the jungle. This, however, did little to discourage the enemy who kept up a hail of fire as I followed the general and his aides sprinting for cover from the landing pad for a pep talk with the defenders.

We were soon airborne again on our way back to Pleiku. Below, we could see the armoured column toiling its way past felled trees and ditches cut by the Viet Cong, and now only about five miles from the besieged camp. This was typical of a situation which was to be repeated over and over again. The Viet Cong would pull back in the face of overwhelming force and then return from the jungle, cut the supply lines and wait in ambush for the relief column.

Already the US military machine was relying more and more on helicopters to take it in and out of battle, rarely staying in a hostile area long enough to clear and secure it. As the war progressed heli-copters became increasingly vulnerable and thousands were destroyed by Viet Cong ground fire.

Shortly before leaving Vietnam I met a rather drunk CIA agent, who was a specialist in Indochina. 'What the f— are we doing here?' he said over a bottle of scotch. 'This is a civil war between the North and South that's been going on for centuries, it's nothing to do with us.' How about the 'Domino Theory' – the then fashionable belief that an American pull-out would deliver South-east Asia to the com-munist bloc – I asked. 'It's all a load of balls,' he replied. 'The moment we leave here, China and the Soviets will be at each other's throats.' He was absolutely right – but no one was listening.

8

Lebanon Revisited

Miles and Nasser

Beirut, after an absence of four years, was booming again. The civil war of 1958 might never have happened, money was pouring in from the Gulf and the Lebanese Christians were becoming prosperous and increasingly confident once more. Unfortunately, prosperity was also devastating the capital and all along the coastline. The charm of the old Mediterranean seaport with its Ottoman, arched stone houses, its sophisticated American University, its French and Arabic restaurants and nightclubs, the unique Levantine atmosphere which subtly combined Paris and Damascus were all being rapidly transformed.

Old Beirut was being torn down to be replaced by high concrete apartment blocks looking like penitentiaries. Huge hotels like the Phoenicia, slap in the middle of the old town, were rising from the rubble of gentle, nineteenth century Ottoman buildings. Much of the charm of the city still survived, but not for long. Prosperity and greed were destroying it as effectively as when it was finally levelled by the guns of the militias over a decade later.

Shortly after we arrived, Miles Copeland told me he was moving to England and suggested we should take over his house. Villa Terazzi was irresistible – a splendid Arabesque building situated just off the Damascus road, inside an olive grove, surrounded by wide balconies overlooking, in the far distance, the Beirut airport and the Mediterranean. It survived during the Lebanese wars of the 1980s as a United Nations headquarters and observation post.

From time to time the water, electricity and phone would fail. And when, not infrequently, the road to Damascus collapsed, all traffic heading from Beirut to Syria, Iraq and Jordan would be diverted down the lane past our house. The landlord, a miserly Syrian antique dealer, claimed, improbably, that he had built the house many years before as a gift of love for his English mistress, the wife of a British army officer.

Thanks to Miles Copeland's reputation, our new home, when we moved in, had become known to the Lebanese as the CIA house. It was many years since Miles had been a CIA agent, but he was never bashful about his links with the agency. While many intelligence agents used business as a cover Miles took a uniquely opposite line – becoming in effect a businessman with CIA cover. As a consultant, chiefly to oil companies, he would stress his intelligence links, real or imagined, to enhance his reputation as the 'man in the know' in the Middle East. One American ambassador in Cairo complained to me that Miles would regularly lie in wait for him after his morning staff meeting, and from the briefest conversation Miles would create a whole fantasy of political theories and events with which to dazzle friends and clients for the rest of the day.

Miles had begun his career in the Office of Strategic Services, the wartime forerunner of the CIA whose acronym became known as Oh.So.Social. because of the upper crust young men it recruited from wealthy East Coast families. But Miles was different. Born in Birmingham, Alabama, he described himself as an old jazz pianist and riverboat gambler. He was generous, outrageous, always fun, never took himself too seriously and had a thoroughly irreverent approach to the intelligence profession. The CIA establishment loathed him for his indiscretions and for his shameless exploitation of the Agency for his own interests.

Back in Britain, he wrote books about the cloak and dagger world, one of which he turned into a highly successful game, while his sons started up the rock group 'The Police' and became millionaires. Before he died in 1991 Miles had become the man the British media turned to for an instant and imaginative interpretation of the latest spy story in the news.

Miles began his career in the Middle East when he was posted to Damascus in the late 1940s under diplomatic cover for the CIA. There he helped engineer a coup which overthrew the Syrian government, replacing it with another just as unstable and unsatisfactory to American interests. Later, while working for an American management consultancy firm, he helped the Egyptians to set up an intelligence agency on similar lines to the CIA. In those days, Gamal Abdel Nasser was deputy prime minister. 'I got to know him well,' Miles used to say. 'He had to come through my office every time he wanted to go for a piss.'

End of an Era

Miles Copeland had been in at the start. By 1965, the UAR had become a state dominated by the intelligence service which largely ran foreign policy. President Nasser, meanwhile, despite the collapse of his union with Syria and his involvement in a disastrous war in the Yemen, was now the unrivalled hero of the Arab World and the most favoured client of the Soviet Union.

It was a time of tremendous activity for Nasser's secret service. Egypt flooded the region with technicians, schoolteachers, doctors and full-time agents – spreading Nasserite influence and subversion throughout the Levant, the Gulf and Africa. Having failed to come to grips with Egypt's domestic problems or to unite the Arab states behind him, President Nasser had turned to the shortcuts of propaganda and subversion to establish himself as the popular leader of the Arabs over the heads of their governments.

On one occasion, I wrote a fairly extensive feature for *The Sunday Telegraph* documenting the activities and world-wide dirty tricks of the United Arab Republic (UAR) secret service – kidnappings, assassinations, sabotage and subversion. Shortly after publication, I found myself, rather uneasily, back in Cairo.

Our garrulous Cairo stringer, Maurice Fahmy, started talking loudly about my article in the taxi from the airport. Taxi-drivers were notoriously government informants and I warned Fahmy that we might be overheard. But Fahmy, who had some connections with Egyptian intelligence, possibly because he had been gaoled by them a few times, told me 'You don't have to worry. They've been making copies of your story to support their claims for a pay raise!'

During my second assignment to the Middle East, I shared the coverage with Eric Downton. We were both based in Beirut, but usually one of us was away in Aden, the Gulf or one of the other Arab states. Under different circumstances, it would have made more sense for one correspondent to be based in Beirut and the other in Cairo, but Cairo's communications were hopeless and the problems were made worse by censorship and visa requirements.

One Western correspondent was subject to an alarming Jekyll and Hyde transformation after a few drinks. He became known among the press corps as 'The Strangler', a name given to him by Don Wise who late one night entered the bar of the Ledra Palace in Nicosia to find him, after a small misunderstanding with the barman, stretching over the counter with his hands round the barman's neck. New members of the press corps were warned by old hands to watch out for a moment in the evening when he began addressing you as 'Doctor'. That was the time to put down your drink and make for the door.

Once, a few of us were sitting in a bar in Baghdad during martial law, when a young Iraqi Air Force officer armed with a Sten gun came in and asked to see our curfew passes. This for some reason infuriated the correspondent, who lunged at the Iraqi and tried to seize his gun. They struggled together out through the door while we sat stunned, expecting any moment to hear a shot. But a few minutes later they were back inside, arms round each other, seemingly the best of friends. Dr Jekyll had returned – just in time.

He always referred to Beirut as the best listening post in the Middle East, a remark that caused some amusement because he was rather deaf. When I had anything serious to discuss with him – such as whose turn it was to go to Aden – I would make a point of phoning him up since he seemed to be able to hear perfectly well on the telephone.

The British government, and press, were still obsessed with President Nasser and his ambitions in the region, and Eric and I seemed to spend most of our time covering stories related to this. These included the Egyptian-instigated war in Yemen, UAR efforts to subvert the Kingdom of Saudi Arabia with bombing attacks and arms drops, the threat posed to the Gulf and the West's oil supplies and the worsening situation in Aden where an ever-increasing number of British civilians were being gunned down by Egyptian-backed terrorists. Egyptian agents were also particularly active in Jordan, stirring up Palestinian refugees, especially on the West Bank, then still part of Jordanian territory, against King Hussein.

But Nasser was riding a tiger. His extremist policies and his intoxicating popularity led him to fatal miscalculations – and to a war with Israel which was to destroy him and force the Arabs to seek new heroes for their cause.

In the Six Days' War in June 1967, Israel killed 10,000 Egyptian troops, occupied the Sinai, captured the Golan Heights from Syria, and seized the West Bank from Jordan. But such was Nasser's following that, even after so total a disaster, I watched huge anti-Western riots and demonstrations in Beirut, repeated throughout the capitals of the Arab world, when Nasser threatened to resign.

Three years later he was dead, at the age of 51, and no new popular leader has since emerged to inspire the Arab world.

The New Saviours

When I flew to Khartoum just after the Six Day War to cover a conference of the humiliated leaders of the Arab states, morale had never been lower. It was a moment when a magnanimous gesture from Israel might have begun a peace process. However, such magnanimity was in short supply, and the world had to wait another generation for the Israeli government to conclude that the conquests of the Six Day's War were not a basis for a Middle East peace and to open negotiations with their enemies.

Instead, the Arabs had to look to new saviours. Realising that they could not compete with Israeli military technology, they pinned their hopes on militant new guerrilla movements to lead the struggle against Israel. The guerrilla warfare waged by the Palestine liberation groups instantly fired their imagination, and they soon believed as fervently in the Palestine liberation groups as they had done in President Nasser. Yasser Arafat was among the more moderate leaders of the new *feddayin* (commando), movements – whose operations against Israel immediately began to destabilise both Jordan and Lebanon.

I was soon to witness the results. Within a few months, the Jordan valley was swarming with Arab guerrillas, beyond the control of King Hussein, staging terrorist attacks across the Israeli frontier. I was in Amman the day the first big Israeli counter-offensive, which became known as the Battle of Karame, was staged in the form of an attack against guerrilla training camps and bases in the Jordan valley with war planes, artillery, tanks and infantry.

An United Press International (UPI) colleague and I picked up a taxi in Amman and, avoiding military checkpoints on the main road, managed to get down to the Jordan valley by a back route. Until holes started appearing in the road about 50 yards in front of the taxi we had not realised we were being strafed. We leapt out and took refuge in a ditch near an Arab Legion anti-aircraft unit, who in great spirits, were firing wildly at a silver line of Israeli *Mirage* fighters stacked up above, as one by one they came screaming down at us.

During a lull we made our way back up the mountain for a bird's eye view of the battle in the valley below. We passed groups of fleeing Palestinian commandos in camouflage battle dress, heavily armed with grenades hanging from their belts, but showing no enthusiasm for the fight.

I learned later from correspondents based in Israel that at dawn they had been escorted by the Israeli Army to the Allenby Bridge where they were to have crossed into Jordan to witness a set-piece Israeli offensive. However, for a change things did not go well for the Israeli forces who ran into much tougher resistance from the Jordanian army than they had anticipated. The newsmen were kept all day on the Israeli side of the frontier and then sent back to Jerusalem. Instead of seeing victorious Israeli troops sweeping the Jordan valley, they watched helicopters flying back Israeli casualties and damaged Israeli tanks being towed back over the Bridge.

A captured Israeli tank was set up in the main square of Amman to celebrate the army's success. The Arab Legion had fought well and the commandos, up against disciplined Israeli troops, had done poorly. But such was the public capacity for self-delusion that the day was celebrated by the crowds as a great victory for the Palestinian freedom fighters, and the key role played by the army was ignored.

Rapidly the Palestinian commandos – Arafat's *Al Fatah* movement and the more extreme Popular Front for the Liberation of Palestine – became a state within a state, taking control of the Jordan valley and setting up military checkpoints all over the country. Finally, three years later King Hussein, driven to desperation, unleashed his Bedouin regiments against the Palestinian guerrillas, killing thousands and expelling the rest from Jordan.

Things were developing in the same way in Lebanon, where the situation further deteriorated when Arafat's forces, thrown out of Jordan, established themselves there. During our last year in the Middle East, the Lebanese Army was fast losing control and the Lebanese Christians were building up their own private armies to oppose the Palestine Liberation Organisation – who were recruiting thousands of Palestinian Moslems from the refugee camps. For the Lebanese Christians the Palestinians became the enemy and Israel, with whom Lebanon was still officially at war, came to be viewed as an ally.

The prospects for Lebanon were already beginning to look bleak when, towards the end of 1968, I was posted to Washington. Eric Downton kindly asked us round for a farewell dinner at his apartment. It overlooked Beirut's corniche road and was next door to the British Embassy, outside which a small bomb had exploded the day before. I therefore viewed the invitation with some slight apprehension, but the dinner passed pleasantly and without incident. When Eric came down to the street late at night to see us off, we saw two men getting out of my car which was parked outside and walking swiftly away.

They turned out to be Lebanese security men sent to keep an eye on the Embassy who had decided to sit in my car to keep out of the cold. Eric was not to know this. Shouting 'spies, saboteurs!' at the top of his voice, he thundered on the door of the startled concierge who then called the police, and within moments we heard the sirens of police cars followed by those of the anti-terrorist Squad Sixteen brandishing sub-machine-guns. Lights appeared from the whole apartment block and, as Eric gesticulated to the growing number of security forces, he inadvertently knocked to the pavement Waff Gillett, a middle-aged lady who was manager of the Reuters' office and one of our fellow guests. We left behind a scene of chaos. Once again, Eric had not failed to live up to expectations.

The day before our departure 28 December 1968, was the day that in many people's view marked the beginning of the disintegration of Lebanon. That night, hearing distant explosions from the airport, I drove there to witness a scene of devastation. As a reprisal against Palestinian terrorist attacks, the Israeli Army had landed by helicopter at Beirut International Airport and had blown up 13 airliners which were still blazing on the runway.

Not a shot had been fired by Lebanese forces against the attackers and back in Beirut the population seemed totally unconcerned. Nightclubs and restaurants were packed but on the outskirts of the city armed and uniformed Palestinians were stopping cars and checking identity papers.

Our last night in Lebanon had been a foretaste of the Israeli invasion and the years of civil strife that over the next two decades was to inflict on Beirut such devastation that this beautiful old city was left looking like a survivor of the Second World War.

9

Washington

Like Old Times

Standing in the middle of an angry crowd in Pennsylvania Avenue, a block down the street from our bureau, was like being back in the Arab world covering yet another anti-American demonstration. The 'Stars and Stripes' was on fire, there was smoke and tear gas in the air, and riot police and troops were struggling with demonstrators screaming curses against the policies of the American government. In their midst was Tom Streithorst, an old colleague from the Middle East, with an NBC television team who, spotting me, shouted out 'hey Dick, just like old times!'

But this was not another Arab demonstration. It was the inauguration of the 37th President of the United States, Richard Milhous Nixon, amid scenes never before witnessed in this normally respectful American ritual. 'One, two, three, four, we don't want your f–ing war!' screamed crowds of long-haired Americans of draft age, many wearing combat fatigues and bizarre, look-alike Nixon masks.

It must have been a depressing scene for President Nixon at his moment of greatest triumph. But he stood up in his limousine giving the crowds a defiant 'V' sign – a two-finger gesture that was to symbolise his administration – as he drove to the White House to begin his ill-fated presidency.

I had arrived in Washington just at the end of the transition period between the Johnson and Nixon administrations. President Johnson had been destroyed by the Vietnam War and Richard Nixon was about to face the same pressures. As *The Washington Post*'s David Broder warned at the time 'the men and the movement that broke Lyndon Johnson's authority in '68 are out to break Richard Nixon in '69'.

America was in a wretched state – divided as never before since the civil war – with its capital city still shattered by the black riots that followed the assassination of Martin Luther King. Only a few months earlier Washington had been under curfew with tanks and armoured cars in the streets. For miles up 14th Street from *The Daily Telegraph* office in the National Press Building, houses, shops, gas stations and liquor stores had been looted and burned. All of black, downtown Washington, with its bars and jazz clubs, had become a sullen, dangerous no-go area for whites, and for that matter continues to remain a ghetto dominated by drugs and gang warfare even today.

During the three years since I had visited Vietnam, the anti-war movement in the United States had grown out of control. Each month, in body bags, the shattered remains of three or four hundred young Americans were being flown back to Washington to swell the ranks in Arlington National Cemetery. Each night, millions of Americans in their homes watched the carnage on television.

In the early days, when the war had had the patriotic support of most Americans, it was largely the blacks and the poor whites who finished up in Arlington. There were ways for the young of the middle classes, like Dan Quayle and Bill Clinton, to avoid the draft by joining the National Guard or extending their college studies. By 1969, however, with over half a million troops in Vietnam, the draft was plucking out the young of the middle classes. Now it was congressmen and their wives and prosperous white Americans from the suburbs, with sons in Vietnam, who joined the candlelight anti-war vigils around the White House and accompanied the marchers on the Pentagon.

Close-cropped American GIs on leave from the most unpopular of America's wars were mocked and shunned by their contemporaries. The clean-cut young American look of the previous decade was amazingly transformed. Equally conformist, the new look emerged as a shambling, drug-culture, Woodstock 'make love not war' generation rioting in college campuses across the country, who were deeply fearful of ending up in Vietnam.

This was the social scene we encountered, and which had a greater impact on our children than on Moyra and myself. My elder daughter Jennifer, who was 16 at the time told me of her early impressions:

> It was quite shocking, walking down Wisconsin Avenue for the first time, seeing children sitting in the street, handing you flowers – and drugged out of their minds.

We used to go to anti-war demos with American friends and wounded vets in wheelchairs. We just went for fun, we didn't really understand what it was all about. And we did not understand why their brothers, young boys on leave from Vietnam, came back so messed up, behaved so strangely and locked themselves away. They had seen things they couldn't explain to us or their parents. And they were into heavy drugs.

Richard Nixon had been voted in to bring an end to a war in which the Democrats had become so hopelessly entangled, with the loss already of 30,000 American lives. He promised the nation peace with honour but brought no quick-fix solution to the White House.

Declaring 'I will not be the first President of the United States to lose a war', Nixon went on to enlarge the conflict by invading Cambodia and launching an unprecedented bombing campaign against North Vietnam. However, after 26,000 more American deaths and the killing of hundreds of thousands of Indo-Chinese, Nixon would no longer be in the White House to witness his nation's final defeat.

A Hard Slog

Washington DC, the capital of the world's superpower, was, I suppose, the goal of most foreign correspondents as they began their nomadic careers. I had been on the road nearly 20 years when I arrived there with my family, aged 43. But it soon became apparent to me that covering Washington for a daily newspaper was a much harder slog, less rewarding and a good deal less fun than the relatively carefree life of bumming around the Middle East and Africa.

In his diaries Malcolm Muggeridge, who was the *Telegraph* Washington correspondent in 1946, wrote 'I sit with the ticker machine watching it spell out the news, then myself spell out the news to London'. Not much had changed. Washington, for the daily correspondent was, is and has to be largely a rewrite job.

Unlike the East, where you start the day covering Beirut, East Africa or Moscow a reasonable two or three hours ahead of London, in Washington you wake up five hours behind and never really catch up. Newspaper foreign rooms all have clocks clearly stating the current time in the major capital cities of the world. It's all perfectly logical, but time differences are facts that foreign editors and their staff clearly find hard to accept.

Your average foreign editor gets up, takes his train from Orpington and the tube, arrives in his office at 9.30am, scans the wires, holds his first editorial meeting, has a coffee, outlines his foreign coverage schedule for the day and prepares to leave for lunch. And his Washington staff are still in bed! Although the evidence is there on his wall that it is not yet 7am on the East Coast of the United States, foreign editors find it hard to believe that the world-shattering events of the past five hours are unknown to their staff.

Reggie Dale, *The Financial Times* Washington Bureau Chief, in a speech at his farewell party in the 1980s said that the way to bridge this confidence gap was to have a mobile telephone at your bedside. At 5.30am, the phone would ring and an excited voice from the foreign desk would demand your reaction to the startling political changes involving, say, the leadership in Beijing. This may be complete news to you, says Reggie, but never let on. Instead, climb out of bed and start descending the stairs, enquiring over the phone about the weather conditions in England – an irresistible topic for the foreign desk. Quietly open the front door where *The Washington Post*, delivered while it is still dark, is resting in the hedge in the snow.

Still talking about the weather, bring in the paper, brush off the snow, and there you will find the story. 'Well', you say, 'about the events in China, State Department officials, are known to be very concerned about the possible effects on Sino-American relations. . . .' Then you can go back to bed.

Another problem is that at the time you arrive at your bureau, usually as the foreign editor is returning from his lunch, nothing much has really happened in the United States. The president has jogged, the congressmen are on their way to Capitol Hill, and it is still three hours or so before the White House, State Department and Pentagon briefings. The greedy *Telegraph* foreign desk by this time has spotted six or seven stories they want covered, you may have in mind another three or four. All have to be filed within about four hours to get into the first editions – and most have not yet happened.

Apart from preparing advance stories for, say, a Senate vote on the budget, the secretary of state's press conference, a report of a scandal in the White House to be addressed later by the president's spokesman, and so on, you have to keep up to date, monitoring the television morning news shows, gutting the columns of the *New York Times*, *The Washington Post*, *The Washington Times* and *The Wall Street Journal*, as well as streaking through the overnight files of Reuters, AP and UPI.

Throughout the day, you are constantly filing new leads and inserts to the running stories as they develop as well as covering new stories as they crop up. On a heavy news day, this deluge of words never stops until you are reduced to cutting and pasting stories culled from paragraphs cut from the newspapers and the agencies.

By about six in the evening, 11pm London time, excluding sensational new developments, you have usually fed the beast for the day and can raise your head from the desk. This distinctly unglamorous routine, I found, compared unfavourably with the excitements of civil wars or *coups d'état*, interspersed with periods for reflection on Beirut beaches or Nairobi tennis courts.

Georgetown

Settling down in Washington, after Africa and the Middle East, presented the mildest of cultural shocks for Moyra and myself. It is surprisingly beautiful – a city in the trees. From the air, in summertime, you can barely see the buildings through the canopy of leaves.

Crossing the Potomac upstream in early morning, it is not hard to picture a birchbark canoe of Red Indians – or to be politically correct 'Native Americans' – paddling past the partly submerged rocks and into the navigable waters that sweep down to the vast Chesapeake Bay.

It was that part of the river that attracted the first British, mainly Scottish, settlers in the seventeenth century who built Georgetown, now a residential section of Washington DC where we chose to live. Georgetown and its almost identical sister town Alexandria, on the opposite bank of the Potomac in Virginia, began as thriving river ports exporting tobacco to England.

English bricks were shipped as ballast on return voyages and used in the building of the elegant eighteenth century Georgian houses that grace the two towns. Preserved for history, the brick pavements and cobbled, tree-lined streets remind one more of Hampstead Village than the typical United States – which peers across the river from the glass skyscrapers of Arlington, Virginia.

We moved into a small Georgetown house on a row that was once a black slum. It was a hundred yards from Dumbarton Oaks, a substantial estate and birthplace of the United Nations, where Roosevelt and Churchill signed the Atlantic Charter in 1941. Around the corner was a house that in the last century was known as the 'Summer White House'. Presidents and their families would drive the two miles from Pennsylvania Avenue by coach for relief when the heat, humidity and sewage turned the tidal basin behind the White House into a stinking swamp.

Before air-conditioning, the British Embassy gave their staff a hardship, aestivation allowance, to help them escape the discomforts of a Washington summer. After a short, magical spring, Washington takes on the climate of the West African coast. Most days the humidity would build up relentlessly under cloudless skies until we were daily emptying buckets of water from our dehumidifier in the basement. Then would come a deafening, Wagnerian tropical storm, with lashing rain, flooded homes and fallen trees blocking the streets. After the storm the skies would clear and the cycle would start again.

Washington winters are hardly less dramatic. A cold blast from Canada can bring the temperature diving from over 60 degrees Fahrenheit in the morning to below zero in the afternoon. And if this wind from the north happens to meet a warm, wet tropical storm coming up from Florida, snow falls on Washington like blankets of flannel.

It was during an ineffectual attempt with nails and a hammer to try to repair the ravages of a summer storm to our garden fence that I first met our next-door neighbour Abe Fortas. Abe was a former Supreme Court Justice, a gifted musician and also a practical man. Clearly unimpressed with my efforts he reappeared with new planks of wood and a tool kit and in no time at all fixed the fence, while I stood by making encouraging noises.

A few weeks earlier we had seen Washington's news media staked out in front of our neighbour's house covering a scandal that finally brought about Justice Fortas's downfall. In the previous year, at the height of Fortas's career, Lyndon Johnson had even nominated him to be Chief Justice of the United States.

Abe, like Johnson, came from the South, and was just about Johnson's closest friend. Although he was a Jewish liberal progressive, he was, oddly enough, one of the strongest influences on the President for pursuing a military victory in Vietnam. Abe, who was not particularly wealthy, had never wanted to be on the Supreme Court. The formidable Johnson, a man almost impossible to say no to, had bullied him into it. However, Abe's career ended in disgrace with his resignation after the press discovered he had quietly accepted $20,000 from a highly dubious foundation while on the bench of the Supreme Court.

He was personally charming, witty and a generous neighbour. His wife Carol was a tough, petite New Yorker who chain-smoked cigars and was said to be the highest paid tax lawyer in Washington. They gave us an open invitation to their swimming pool – no small blessing in Washington in summertime – and used to ask us to their Sunday musical evenings. There, Abe with a small group of his musician friends, which included Rostropovich, would play his Stradivarius, while we would often sit in the adjoining study listening to the music with Carol as she sipped a bourbon and puffed at a huge Havana cigar. Their kindness and hospitality was typical of the enormous, almost embarrassing goodwill that we found that Americans showed towards English people.

During the 1920s and 1930s, Georgetown had been a sleepy, easy-going, impoverished southern town – largely black in population with a few white-owned, very grand houses. Gradually it became a wealthy, fashionable, all-white district where Jack and Jackie Kennedy lived. Small former slave houses were converted into desirable town houses and sold for fortunes. Almost the only blacks to be seen were house servants.

The 'Georgetown set' during the Cold War became the heart of Washington's foreign-policy establishment and Washington society, comprising many of the nation's leading diplomats, journalists and CIA personnel and politicians. Within a short walk of us, though in much grander circumstances, lived the Dean Achesons, Pamela and Averell Harriman, Kay Graham, the owner of *The Washington Post*, the David Bruces and columnists Scotty Reston, Joe Kraft and Clayton Fritchey.

The dean of the Georgetown set was Joe Alsop – columnist, super Cold War warrior and cousin of the formidable Alice Roosevelt Longworth whose imperious manner gained her the title of 'Princess Alice'. Georgetown was, and still is, a wealthy Democrat-dominated society, shunned by most Republicans who usually lived in garden suburbs across the Potomac. Richard Nixon, partly no doubt from a sense of social inferiority, was inordinately suspicious of Georgetown and its grand dinner parties. And he hated his Secretary of State Henry Kissinger's close relations with the Georgetown set.

Georgetown's prestige and influence reached its height during the Kennedy administration. But we witnessed its decline as the Democratic establishment was torn apart by the Vietnam War and Georgetown itself, with the growing crime rate, became an increasingly dangerous place to live.

Although Washington was more than 70 per cent black, blacks were almost never seen at smart dinner parties – except to change the plates. If one did appear he or she would probably turn out to be a diplomat from an African embassy. It was almost an agreement for apartheid by mutual consent by black and white Washingtonians not to mix socially, and this did not just reflect economic differences.

Apart from the inner-city black ghetto, there has been for generations a large, prosperous black middle-class community in Washington. Most of them live in an extensive area of north-west Washington known to the whites as 'The Goldcoast', leading quite separate lives and largely indifferent to the plight of their desperate compatriots in the ghetto. These black lawyers, doctors and dentists live parallel lives to the wealthy white Washingtonians, but mostly attend their own churches and clubs. Unlike New York or Los Angeles, middle-class blacks and whites in Washington show little inclination to fraternise with each other.

Black–white relations were mostly uneasy and distant. When we first arrived blacks were often still referred to as 'negroes'. Then the correct word became 'black' and when we left it had changed to 'Afro-American'. Blacks among themselves were much more relaxed about political correctness and would frequently greet each other cheerfully as 'hey you mother-f–in' nigger'.

Washington Bureau

Stephen Barber was the *Telegraph* bureau chief when I arrived. The other member of the bureau was Dominick Harrod, son of the economist Sir Roy Harrod, who specialised in economic and financial news coverage before moving on to the BBC.

A recent predecessor of mine in Washington was Jeremy Wolfenden, who had died tragically of drink. Jeremy, a scruffy, brilliant academic, was a Fellow of All Souls and the son of Lord Wolfenden who had produced the 1950s report on homosexuality. Jeremy himself was gay, even before his father's report helped make homosexuality legal. As the *Telegraph*'s Moscow correspondent, he had plenty of gay affairs including one with a Russian hairdresser. The KGB took pictures of him in bed with his boyfriend and then tried to blackmail him into working for them. He informed the British Embassy and British intelligence persuaded him to go along with the KGB demands and act as a double agent.

The pressure of this life led to a near breakdown, and Jeremy, by this time married to an Englishwoman who had been working for the family of a British defence attaché in Moscow, was posted to Washington. But he brought his problems with him. One night after a Christmas party, Steve Barber discovered Jeremy lying unconscious in his bathroom with so much drink inside him that he died hours later in a Washington hospital. He was, to some extent, a victim of the Cold War.

Steve, who had just taken over the bureau when I arrived, had been an assistant editor of the *News Chronicle* when I joined that paper, and, like me, had been taken on by the *Telegraph*. A few years older than me, Steve was brought up in Alexandria, Egypt, joined the AP when he was about 16 and covered some of the Second World War in the Middle East. He was an outrageous character who loved to shock and was always full of youthful enthusiasms, unaffected by middle age.

On the *Chronicle*, for example. he took an elephant over the Alps in the footsteps of Hannibal, with a *vin d'honneur* arranged for each day of the journey. He used to exhaust the plodding *Chronicle* deputy editor Norman Cursley with his ideas so that as soon as Steve returned from a foreign trip, Cursley used to look desperately for another excuse to send him around the world again and get him off his back.

Steve was a normal sized man, but born with short legs and a delicate heart. He compensated for his failure to pass the medical to get into the forces by being a fearless correspondent. 'He was the bravest man I've ever seen' SAS Colonel John Slim who had been with Steve in the Korean War, once told me.

The 'poor man's Randolph Churchill' was how Steve was sometimes unkindly described. He was in fact a friend of Randolph's, much admired him, and they had a similar capacity to outrage and shock. But Steve's rather blimpish manner was largely a pose. While adopting an old-fashioned, upper-class persona, Steve at the same time hated the arrogance, incompetence and unprofessionalism of that all too familiar Establishment Tory from a privileged background.

He was inclined to dismiss the Americans as a lot of 'peasants in motorcars' and often referred to blacks as 'silly sambos'. But his best friend was a black American, and, typically, he elected to be buried in an old slave graveyard in Virginia. Despite his scornful attitude towards Americans he was impressed with the scale and vision of the United States, compared with that of a shrinking, inward-looking little England, which he used to refer to dismissively as 'Toytown'.

When Steve, as a young reporter, was covering the civil war in Greece in the mid-1940s, he met and married a Greek girl, Mary, the daughter of a doctor, who had worked for the wartime resistance. It was said that she married Steve on the rebound from an affair with an American war correspondent and the marriage only lasted a few months. Soon after she returned to Athens to join a junior British diplomat at the Embassy in Athens, Nico Henderson

whom she subsequently married. Steve later married Deirdre, the ex-
wife of Lord Aberconway, and the Barbers were in Washington when
Sir Nicholas Henderson became Ambassador there.

Meanwhile, I had been posted to Moscow, and when Steve died
early in 1980 following a stroke, I was sent back to take over the
Washington Bureau. Shortly after we arrived we were asked to dinner
at the British residence. I was talking to Washington columnist
Clayton Fritchey when Mary Henderson came up to us.

'This is Dick Beeston who has come over to replace Steve Barber'
said Clayton. 'Did you know Steve?'

'I was married to him briefly', replied Mary 'but I am not sure I
ever really knew him.'

Amour Propre

For Western correspondents accustomed to working in the Third
World or the communist bloc, where relations with the host authorities were normally abrasive or downright hostile, Washington came
as something of a shock. Stories filed from, say Africa, the Middle
East or the Soviet Union, received the closest attention from the
local authorities and could have, to say the least, inconvenient consequences. The slightest hint of criticism could provoke angry
threats from the government, or a personal attack in the government-
controlled press. On several occasions during my career I was
expelled or declared *persona non grata*, and a colleague in the Soviet
Union, whose coverage infuriated the government, was even poisoned by the KGB and very nearly died.

They view things differently in America, however. The overriding
interest of The White House is to get its president re-elected, and
therefore, a reporter from the remotest regional rag rates higher
than the grandest of correspondents from the overseas press.
Occasionally, perhaps on the eve of a presidential visit to Europe,
the correspondents of papers from countries on the White House
itinerary are wheeled in for a presidential briefing. The rest of the
time they are largely ignored and no one bothers to read what they
write.

This attitude is largely reflected by the American reader in general.
The Daily Telegraph, for example, a notorious target in the Third
World as representing the right wing of the imperialist press, is practically unknown in the United States except as a defunct American
racing newspaper. Oddly enough, probably the best known British
newspaper title in the States is the *Manchester Guardian*.

It therefore often comes as quite a blow to a foreign correspondent's self-esteem (normally fairly considerable) when first posted to the United States, to encounter a distressing lack of interest in who he is or what he writes. One French correspondent from *Le Figaro*, after a long and turbulent period in Moscow, was so upset by the indifference in Washington to his presence and his views that he applied to go back to the Soviet Union, where he was again followed, bugged and harassed, but where he felt that at least he was being taken seriously!

Chappaquiddick

Nineteen sixty-nine, my first year in Washington, saw the rapid build-up of the anti-war movement – and with it the growing paranoia of Richard Nixon that was to lead to his destruction.

On the face of it, the year was not altogether a bad one for the Nixon administration. There were still a lot of Americans prepared to give Nixon a chance to bring peace with honour, and the violence, the flag burning and the obscenities of the riots and demonstrations in the streets and campuses created a backlash that he was quick to exploit.

Spiro Agnew, the administration's crooked Vice President, was given the task of mobilising the conservatives by appealing to the patriotism of Americans dubbed by Nixon 'the Silent Majority'. Agnew did a good job in attacking the draft dodgers, the long-haired demonstrators and the 'limousine liberals' of the Democratic establishment. He struck a chord with the blue-collar and middle-class Norman Rockwell Americans, accustomed to respecting flag and country. It then became the fashion among Nixon supporters to demonstrate their patriotism by wearing a small stars and stripes badge in their lapels.

In that year Richard Nixon had another political windfall when Senator Ted Kennedy left his secretary Mary Jo Kopechne to drown in a creek in Chappaquiddick, Martha's Vineyard, effectively eliminating himself as Nixon's most serious rival to the White House. The previous year Kennedy, aged 36, was, according to a Gallup Poll, one of the three most admired men in the United States. But for his disgrace on Martha's Vineyard, he could well have won the presidential election in 1972, or if not then, in 1976, and the course of history would certainly have been altered.

But despite all the efforts of the rich and powerful supporters of the Kennedy clan to rebuild their candidate, the albatross of

Chappaquiddick clung to Ted Kennedy, destroying his final, hopeless bid for the presidency in 1980.

Paranoia

The albatross around Richard Nixon's own neck, of course, was the Vietnam War – a war which he had inherited from the Democrats who were now distancing themselves from his efforts to extricate America from its increasingly disastrous involvement.

'North Vietnam cannot defeat or humiliate the United States. Only Americans can do that', Nixon declared, ignoring the advice of one senator that the US should simply declare victory in Vietnam and pull out. But Nixon was convinced that, through his policy of 'Vietnamisation', he could build up a strong South Vietnam able to withstand the North without American forces, thus preventing his 'humiliation' and the consequences of the 'Domino Theory' which forecast the collapse of pro-Western nations in South-east Asia if Hanoi won.

In this belief, Nixon was aided and abetted by a Briton, Sir Robert Thompson, at one time his favourite adviser on Vietnam War strategy. Thompson, who used to make frequent visits to the White House and toured Vietnam on Nixon's behalf, had been a counter-terrorism expert during the communist insurgency in Malaya.

Despite a totally different set of circumstances, Thompson managed to convince Nixon of a parallel between the two wars, asserting that the Vietnam War too could be won by winning the support of the South Vietnamese people against the Viet Cong. He even went so far as to warn Nixon that 'The future of Western civilisation is at stake in the way you handle yourself in Vietnam.'

In the first years of his administration Nixon did succeed in substantially reducing American forces in Vietnam. In other ways, too, things were looking up. Chappaquiddick had eliminated his biggest rival. And in those early years Richard Nixon had enjoyed the prestige of presiding over man's first landing on the moon. Diplomatically, he had displayed a brilliant and daring grasp of international affairs with his nuclear arms negotiations in Moscow and his spectacular visit to China.

But just as character weaknesses had destroyed Ted Kennedy's political career, it was the flaws in Nixon's own character that were the direct cause of Watergate – America's biggest political scandal.

On becoming President, Nixon had promised to bring the nation together. But he was a lonely, suspicious, insecure and vengeful man.

He had won the presidency against Hubert Humphrey in 1968 by a whisker and his re-election by a thumping victory over George McGovern in 1972. However, with the growth of the anti-war movement, huge demonstrations in the capital and violence and unrest throughout the college campuses of the United States, Nixon began to retreat behind his 'Berlin Wall' within the White House. One morning, on my daily walk along Pennsylvania Avenue to our bureau, I saw the entire White House encircled bumper to bumper by police buses, a laager against anti-war demonstrators and the outside world.

Holed up inside the White House, with Chief of Staff HR Haldeman the grim keeper of the gates, and the duplicitous National Security Adviser Henry Kissinger playing Iago to his fears and suspicions, the darker side of Richard Nixon's personality was given free rein.

Looked down upon by cultivated Americans as a social inferior, without small talk or social graces, Nixon was stiff and awkward and unable even to relax with his own family. He was almost friendless except for two improbable close chums, both millionaires and contributors to Republican funds, Bebe Rebozo and Robert Abplanalp.

Whenever he could take a weekend off, Nixon used to board Air Force One to Key Biscayne, Florida, to be with Bebe and Bob – and I would frequently fly down on the White House press plane along with a few hundred other reporters, photographers and television teams equipped with swimming shorts and tennis rackets.

It was Nixon's idea of relaxation to spend hours and hours aboard a small houseboat with Rebozo, a Cuban-born Miami banker, and Abplanalp, the multi-millionaire inventor of the aerosol valve, playing poker, drinking and using the below-deck language of his US Navy days. It was on such a weekend – 17 June 1972 – that Nixon first learned of the break-in of the Democratic National Committee headquarters at the Watergate building in Washington and commented 'It's the dumbest thing I've ever heard of.'

Like most papers, we reported the story in a few paragraphs on an inside page – a political prank, just another bizarre example of the dirty tricks of American politics.

Watergate

At that moment, as a Washington correspondent, I could never have predicted that for the next two years my life, and the lives of my colleagues, would become completely dominated by Watergate – the biggest political scandal of the century.

Like most of Richard Nixon's troubles, the Watergate scandal that was to destroy him had its origins in Vietnam. At the height of his paranoia, sitting in his beleaguered White House, Nixon became obsessed about leaks to the media of policy secrets over Vietnam. He was in particular outraged by the *New York Times* publication of a top-secret Defence Department study – the Pentagon Papers – revealing the US government's concealment of its increasing military involvement in Indochina. In an effort to plug the leaks the White House secretly recruited the 'Plumbers', so named because they were supposed to plug government leaks. They were a wildly incompetent break-in gang of Cuban exiles, headed by two Americans with links to the FBI and the CIA.

President Nixon became obsessed with the man who leaked the Pentagon papers, Daniel Ellsberg, a former hawkish Pentagon aide who changed sides and became a leading critic of the Vietnam War. Nixon saw him as an ally of Ted Kennedy who was providing him with ammunition to oppose Nixon's strategy for pursuing the war.

E Howard Hunt, an eccentric retired CIA agent, recruited the Plumbers from among Cuban exiles with whom he had been involved in the disastrous Bay of Pigs invasion of Cuba. In an effort to smear Ellsberg, and if possible Kennedy, Nixon sanctioned a break-in of the California office of Ellsberg's psychiatrist. 'I want it done whatever the cost', Nixon told Chief of Staff Haldeman.

There had been rumours that Ellsberg took drugs and indulged in peculiar sexual habits. With the hope of finding evidence of this, the Plumbers searched the psychiatrist's office for Ellsberg's files. Typically, they failed to find them, and so ransacked the office to try to make it look like a burglary. From the start, the CIA was compromised by having to supply Hunt and his ex-FBI colleague Gordon Liddy with disguises and false identification.

The Plumbers then engaged in other White House dirty tricks enterprises with equal lack of success, but requiring secret funding to pay their salaries and expenses. As their final disaster, it was this gang, working for the sinisterly named CREEP – the Committee to re-elect the President – who broke into the Watergate headquarters of the Democratic National Committee on 16 June 1972. Their mission was to plant bugs and search for salacious material, including addresses of call-girls thought to be having affairs with Democrats, in order to discredit the Democratic election campaign. After the five Plumbers were caught red-handed and arrested the White House spokesman Ron Zeigler brushed off the whole affair as 'a third-rate burglary'. The story soon hit the headlines, however, when one of the gang was found to have an address file with the entry 'H Hunt WH' and a phone number. The number turned out to be Howard Hunt's.

The cover-up to the Watergate break-in began immediately as White House aides quickly removed the incriminating contents of Hunt's office safe which included a revolver and ammunition, a folder on Ellsberg, another on Ted Kennedy and an address book. At that point the press – accustomed to dirty tricks by both political parties – had failed to recognise the dimension of the story. But the immediate problem for the White House was how to raise huge sums of money to buy the silence of the arrested Watergate burglars and get them to accept their inevitable gaol sentences. Above all Watergate must not be allowed to jeopardise Nixon's election later that year.

At first, Nixon's White House Counsel John Dean tried unsuccessfully to persuade the CIA to provide the 'hush money' from its secret funds. The money, including a first payment of nearly half a million dollars, was finally taken illegally from donations to re-elect the President fund and on August 29, Nixon told a news conference that he could state 'categorically' that no one in the White House staff and no one in the administration had taken part in 'this bizarre incident' and that John Dean had made a complete investigation of the affair.

In November Nixon, despite the ever-gathering Watergate storm clouds, was re-elected by a landslide victory, his prestige boosted by the success of his visits to Beijing and Moscow. His Democratic opponent George McGovern won only two states – Massachusetts and the District of Columbia. The irony of Watergate was that Nixon need not have worried about the Democrat election challenge. He was already home and dry.

I attended an election party in Georgetown as the votes were coming in. Most of the guests were Republican supporters and a few of them were from the CIA. They were all clearly elated by the victory and when I raised the issue of Watergate, no one appeared the slightest bit concerned!

As the crime and the resulting White House cover-up took on a life of their own, the characters in the drama became household names on both sides of the Atlantic: professional tough guy G Gordon Liddy who specialised in holding his hand over a flaming candle: the brusque Attorney-General John Mitchell, who went to gaol, and his tragic, alcoholic and loquacious wife Martha; southern, homespun senator Sam Ervin, chairman of the Watergate committee; Bob Woodward and Carl Bernstein, *The Washington Post*

Watergate team; baby-faced White House Counsel John Dean who betrayed his boss and blew wide open the presidential cover-up conspiracy; and Archibald Cox, the Watergate Special Prosecutor.

Nixon barely had time to celebrate his victory before the storm broke. Within days of the election, the Senate, scenting blood, had called for the Senate Judiciary Committee to conduct 'a complete and impartial investigation' into the scandal led by Sam Ervin. Nixon's second term began in January 1973 and for the next 20 months Watergate was the unending story that resulted in the first resignation in history of a US President.

In those pre-computer days, we were all glued to our typewriters, covering congressional investigations, court hearings and the latest revelations of 'deep throat', as Nixon ducked and twisted in his efforts to conceal his part in the cover-up. Always hanging over his head was the fear that the Plumbers, who had now gone on trial before tough, no-nonsense Judge John Sirica, would accept the judge's offer of mild sentences if they cooperated and revealed who hired them. By this time Howard Hunt had begun to blackmail the White House for more money and Nixon, in one of the most damaging of the White House tapes, asks John Dean how much money is required. Dean tells him a million dollars and Nixon replies 'We could get that . . . you could get a million dollars. And you could get it in cash. I, I know where it could be gotten.'

Unknown to Nixon, Dean was already considering defecting to save his own skin. On 15 April, Nixon learned that Dean had been involved in plea bargaining to win immunity from prosecution, for testimony naming Haldeman, Erlichman, Mitchell and others in the cover-up. At that point Nixon must have realised that he would have to sacrifice his 'President's Men' in order to survive and most of them paid the price by going to gaol.

In June, before the Senate Watergate committee Dean, accompanied by his striking blonde wife Maureen, testified for the first time that Nixon had been involved in the pay-off of Hunt's blackmail and that the President had continued the cover-up after he had called on Nixon to remove 'the cancer on the Presidency'.

Nixon's fate was, however, sealed in July 1973 when an obscure civil servant, Alexander Butterfield, testified to the Ervin Committee that the President had had the White House bugged for his own records. This sensational news exposed one of the best-kept secrets of the administration – that almost all of Nixon's White House conversations since 1971 had been taped – and transformed the Watergate investigation.

One of the few people who had earlier rumbled the secret was the former British prime minister Sir Alex Douglas-Home. In his book *Nixon: A Life*, Jonathan Aitken reveals that Douglas-Home and the British Ambassador Lord Cromer, at a meeting in the Oval Office, noticed that neither Nixon nor Henry Kissinger were taking any notes of the discussions. Douglas-Home asked Cromer to check with MI6, who were able to confirm that the White House was indeed bugged and that their conversations were being recorded.

Had Nixon taken the decision after Butterfield's testimony to destroy the tapes he might have got away with it. However, he was in hospital recovering from pneumonia at the time of this crucial revelation. He held a bedside meeting with his aides – some recommended the tapes should be instantly burned, but others argued that such destruction of evidence could lead to impeachment. Nixon hesitated and probably lost his last chance of surviving the Watergate scandal. Both the Ervin Committee and the Watergate Special Prosecutor Archibald Cox demanded to be allowed to listen to the relevant tapes, but Nixon refused on the grounds of executive privilege. This set off a long legal battle between the White House and Congress which was to last a year, dominating the news and virtually crippling the administration.

Two new blows to the presidency followed. Vice President Spiro Agnew, who had managed to stay clear of the Watergate affair found himself involved in his own scandal. Caught taking bribes, handed over in plain envelopes in his White House office, Agnew, a badly flawed but popular figure among Nixon's right-wing supporters, was given a three-year suspended gaol sentence and forced to resign. At the same time, Nixon became involved in his own financial problems when the Internal Revenue Service published details showing Nixon had been underpaying on his income tax by over $400,000.

The story broke just before Nixon was due to deliver a speech in, of all places, Disney World in Florida. I flew down with the White House press corps to cover the event and heard him proclaim 'People have got to know whether or not their President is a crook. Well, I am not a crook.' The 'I Am Not A Crook' headlines in next day's paper were just about as bad publicity as anything that had so far come out from Watergate.

Flailing around desperately as his opponents closed in, Nixon caused a new sensation in the so-called 'Saturday night massacre' by firing the Watergate Special Prosecutor Archibald Cox and taking himself another step towards impeachment. The following day, as I walked past the White House, demonstrators were holding up placards calling on motorists to 'Honk for impeachment'. And most of them seemed to be doing so.

Congress also seemed to take notice. Democrats began calling for impeachment proceedings and Republicans made it clear that they would not oppose the process unless Nixon delivered up the tapes.

After the dismissal of Archibald Cox, Nixon, under growing pressure, made the sensational decision of agreeing to release some of the Watergate tapes. He also appointed a new Watergate Special Prosecutor, an eminent Texas lawyer, Leon Jaworski. By December 1973, after having listened to the tapes, Jaworski told General Alexander Haig, the new White House Chief of Staff, that Nixon should get the finest criminal lawyer he could find.

As more and more of the tapes were grudgingly released to the public, Americans all over the nation, Democrats and Republicans were stunned at the coarseness of the language used by Nixon and his top aides, and of the cynicism and bitterness of their discussions, reminiscent of a meeting of mafia bosses. By this time Nixon had very few supporters left on Capitol Hill.

Finally, in June 1974 the House Judiciary Committee voted to impeach the President. After reviewing the evidence, throughout six days of televised debate, the Committee reached its verdict that Nixon had obstructed justice and should be impeached and removed from office.

The final evidence of presidential obstruction in the case was the release of the so-called 'smoking gun' tape of 23 June 1972, in which Chief of Staff Haldeman tells the President that they must get the CIA to tell the FBI to 'stay the hell out' of investigating Watergate.

Nixon's brisk reply 'Right, fine' was the evidence needed to prove his obstruction of justice and lead to Nixon's resignation to avoid criminal trial. As soon as his intention to resign became known, bewildered crowds gathered outside the White House. On 8 August he made a defiant resignation speech in which he failed to admit any wrongdoing and without ever mentioning impeachment. The next day Nixon's successor, Vice President Gerald Ford, who had replaced Spiro Agnew, became president and proclaimed 'Our long national nightmare is over'. He later granted Nixon a full pardon 'for all offenses against the United States'.

Richard Nixon had brilliant gifts to offer his nation as a world statesman but was destroyed by the demons of suspicion and insecurity. An even more tragic figure was his unfortunate wife Pat, whom I saw countless times standing beside her husband, as she had done from the start in all the ups and downs of his ambitious career, desperately shy, a strained, blank face, and obviously hating every moment of it. Although he clearly depended on her being there, Nixon was so emotionally inhibited that in public he was never able to extend his arm to her or show a gesture of affection.

Two years after their exile to San Clemente, Pat suffered a stroke, said to have occurred after reading her portrayal as a drunken recluse in the book *The Final Days* by Woodward and Bernstein. Nixon, against all odds, gradually emerged as a respected elder statesman whose views were sought by his successors – a man who seemed to have come to terms with his demons.

'Honey, I forgot to duck'

A large Bloody Mary at dawn, handed to you as you board the White House charter jet, frequently starts a Washington correspondent's working day. One of the regular chores is to cover the President wherever he travels – criss-crossing the nation in his never-ending campaign for re-election, or circling the earth to enhance his domestic and international reputation.

Just after the Second World War there were only a handful of regular White House correspondents, but now there are several thousand with White House accreditation. The majority of these are television teams, reporters, producers, cameramen and technicians, as well as a minority of old-fashioned newspaper and wire service correspondents.

To accommodate this media circus, the White House charters as many airliners as required to follow the progress of the president. Aboard Air Force One, a small, select pool accompanies the president. The rest of us convert our chartered airliner into a sort of airborne cocktail party and temporary home for a journey which might last a week on election coverage or overseas trips.

Departure is from Andrews Airbase near Washington – the Doomsday airport from which the president is supposed, if he is quick enough off the mark, to exit in advance of a nuclear attack. Clutching the first drink of the day we stand chatting in the aisles on take-off, regardless of safety regulations, conscious that we are the world's most pampered of air travellers.

Throughout the flights we are handed advances of the presidential speeches. Buses meet us at our destination to take us to the press centres, usually sports stadiums or conference halls, where closed circuit television covers the presidential address. Recordings of the speeches are played on the coaches to us as we are driven back to the plane, where champagne and lunch awaits us. Copies of pool reports from those following the president are distributed throughout the day and night, and it is quite common to cover a complete tour without even a live sighting of him.

On trips abroad we are driven directly to and from the plane, oblivious of airport security or passport control. Arriving at our hotel our bags are delivered straight to our rooms. Usually the most traumatic moment of the tour is its termination after midnight at Andrews. There, one struggles out into the real world to search for luggage and transport, by then expecting to be greeted at home with a drink, a smile and a three-course meal.

Sometimes one covers events in four or five states in a day until you forget where you have been and where you are going. During week-long election stints the plane becomes a sort of chaotic family. People wander in and out of the flight deck, airline hostesses sit on the laps of passengers and crew and there is a lot of massaging of necks and backs. During the trip the gossip builds up as new relationships are established – about who saw a television correspondent leaving the suite of the President's National Security Adviser to return to her hotel room in the early hours of the morning.

However, despite the camaraderie, and the fact that we all pay first-class plus fares for our seats, there is a clear pecking order. Cameramen and technicians are kept in the back of the plane in the tourist section, while millionaire television anchormen and bureau chiefs from the most senior US newspapers, always allocated first-class seats, rarely mix with their less celebrated colleagues.

One naturally longs for some unscheduled incident to break the monotony of almost identical speeches delivered in state after state. Richard Nixon could usually whistle up a storm of scruffy anti-Vietnam War protesters in confrontations that he seemed to enjoy. His successor Gerald Ford had to be closely watched because of a tendency to fall over or slip down the steps of the aircraft. Although a top-class footballer in his day, Ford was surprisingly ill-coordinated, giving rise to the report that he could not jog and chew gum at the same time.

President Jimmy Carter was an earnest, dreary man to cover, who seemed to lower the temperature all round. His style was summed up for me during the 1980 European Economic Summit when our first stop was Rome. Much to the surprise of the Italians he had never before visited their capital and was offered an evening with all the city had to offer. His choice was an early night – preceded by a jog around the Quirinale.

Carter had a depressing effect on Americans. Ronald Reagan was the exact opposite, which was probably why he was elected. Dismissed by his critics as a dim, B-rated movie actor, he had tremendous presence and magnetism which you could see quite clearly working on even people least prepared to like or admire him. Unlike Carter, he made people feel good. And he looked good, an all-American hero from the West, walking tall, delivering a tear-jerking speech on the Normandy beaches or a witty, spontaneous one-liner. 'It's the oddest thing and true even if everyone says it,' states Peggy Noonan, a Reagan speechwriter. 'It is not possible to be nervous in his presence. He acts as if he is lucky to be with you.'

After the spate of assassinations in the 1960s, the possibility of an attempt on the President's life was a permanent consideration in covering the White House. After a long day following President Ford around California I was sitting in a press bus outside a San Francisco hotel waiting to go to the airport when a woman fired a shot as Ford was entering his limousine.

I could just see the woman in the crowd being overpowered by the police as the presidential motorcade took off in a panic, speeding through the city heading for a remote US airbase where Air Force One and the press planes were waiting. It was about 5pm – one o'clock in the morning in London and just time to get the presidential assassination attempt story into the *Telegraph*'s last editions. But it was impossible to leave the bus, or to file once aboard the plane which was returning to Washington.

There was, however, a solitary phone kiosk beside our plane in the midst of a vast, deserted military airfield. As everyone boarded for a hurried takeoff, I set myself up in the phone booth and with the help of eye-witness reports on my transistor radio filed a fairly complete story to London. Unfortunately, by the time I had finished all the planes had left and I found myself alone and abandoned on the empty airstrip. But in the far distance I could see the dust from an approaching truck which stopped beside me, loaded on the phone booth and took me back to San Francisco.

The next presidential assassination attempt was five years later in 1981 after I had returned to Washington from Moscow. I was taking a morning off for a game of squash with a British doctor, Oliver Alabaster, in the basement of the George Washington hospital where he worked. We finished the game just as Reagan's motorcade arrived with the President close to death after being shot in the chest by John Hinckley. Long before the press arrived outside the hospital, my doctor friend was questioning his colleagues about Reagan's condition, while I was on the phone to London.

Despite a bullet lodged an inch from his heart, Reagan performed his best role. 'Please tell me you're Republicans,' he said to the surgeons and nurses preparing for the operation. And to his distraught wife Nancy he quipped 'Honey, I forgot to duck.'

Move to Moscow

It was in the early days of the Carter administration that the phone woke us up at about five in the morning – coffee time at the *Telegraph* – with a call from London. Ricky Marsh, the Foreign Editor, wanted to know if I would staff Moscow and needed an answer in two hours before he met 'The Proprietor' – as Lord Hartwell was reverentially referred to. As we could not get back to sleep, we had a brief chat and within the hour phoned London and said yes.

The family had all enjoyed living in Washington, but now with Fiona and Richard at school in England and Jennifer at university in Scotland, the decision was easier to make. We had met many American corespondents returning to Washington after a stint in the Soviet Union and were under no illusions about how difficult life was likely to be.

A few years earlier Peter Eastwood, the Managing Editor, as part of an economy campaign, had unwisely decided to shut down the Moscow bureau and give up our apartment and office there. The *Telegraph* had since been covering the Soviet Union with reporters sent out from London. However, Moscow had now started to get difficult and had just denied us a visa to cover a Moscow visit by a British government delegation – although the Soviet authorities naturally detested *The Daily Telegraph*, they were at the same time piqued that a leading British newspaper, with seven correspondents in the United States, should not even be accredited to Moscow. When we protested about the denial of visas we were told there would be no change in policy unless we reopened our Moscow bureau.

Foreign coverage was always a top priority with the *Telegraph* and Lord Hartwell hated, above all, being prevented from sending in his correspondents to cover the news. So, overriding Eastwood he ordered the immediate reopening of the Moscow bureau.

Accommodation in Moscow was almost impossible to find. It was illegal to rent privately and you were only allowed to deal through a huge, corrupt, government office – the Diplomatic Corps Service Bureau controlled by the KGB and to my knowledge, no newspaper, except for the *Telegraph*, had ever voluntarily given up its hard-won accommodation in Moscow. Everyone stuck to their inadequate, cockroach-infested flats – which however looked like palaces to the ordinary Russian. Aware of the problems involved, I persuaded the *Telegraph* to give the posting a six-month trial period. If we were still without accommodation after that time, it was agreed I should return to Washington.

With pressure to open up Moscow as soon as possible, we had little time to learn Russian, but for a few weeks we were taught the basics of the language by an aristocratic Serbian lady, Kosara Gavrilovitch, the daughter of the last royalist Yugoslav ambassador to Moscow. Kosara despised the communists in Moscow and Belgrade, but was passionately attached to the Serbs and their orthodox church.

Some of the Russian phrases she taught us seemed to have disappeared with the Bolshevik Revolution and produced puzzled looks in Moscow. Our first lesson was based on a Russian children's book about a roguish, capitalist crocodile who wore a long fur coat and smoked long *papirosy*, paper-stemmed Russian cigarettes. I could find no trace of the book in Moscow, it presumably being deemed unsuitable for the children of the Revolution.

Just before leaving for the Soviet Union, Nicholas Elliott, the former MI6 director whose career had been clouded by his close friendship with Kim Philby, dropped in for lunch and a chat. Inevitably, the conversation turned to Philby, who had barely been seen since his defection, and to speculation as to whether I might meet him again. 'What would you do if you met him?' I asked Nicholas, very much the polite, affable Etonian, who had championed Philby long after most people had turned their backs on him. 'If I had my chance, I would put my hands round his neck and strangle him,' said Elliott. But I could not help feeling that Nicholas would have come off second best in the encounter.

It was Elliott's idea that when Philby died, in order to confuse the KGB, he should be appointed a CMG, and that Nicholas should write in his obituary that Philby was one of the bravest men he had ever known. 'This', suggested Elliott, 'would cause terrific trouble in the Lubyanka!'

Another friend of ours in Washington who had suffered from his friendship with Kim Philby was James Jesus Angleton, the CIA's Head of Counter Intelligence. Jim Angleton liked the British, had attended an English public school and had worked for American intelligence in the OSS in London during the war. Tall, thin and owlish, he looked a little like T S Eliot – and indeed was himself a poet. He had fallen under Philby's spell when Kim was the SIS representative in Washington in the 1950s. The two lunched every week at Harvey's restaurant, shared a liking for large quantities of martinis and dined at each other's houses.

Angleton was a night owl, and he used to visit us in Georgetown late in the evenings, happily staying on until dawn unless he could be persuaded to leave. He used to claim to me that he was the first to suspect Kim. However, it is clear from the records that the man who first fingered Philby as a Soviet spy was an FBI agent, Bill Harvey, whose wife Philby had insulted at a drunken party at Philby's house in Washington. For a time, even after the Burgess and Maclean defections, Angleton continued to defend Philby to the CIA, but when he realised he had been duped, he was devastated and his suspicions of the KGB reached paranoia.

Single-handedly, he devastated the CIA in his fruitless search for a mole – an American Philby. Finally, CIA director Admiral Stansfield Turner fired him and he was given as a farewell present a large, rather sinister-looking black Mercedes which he used to park outside our house on his late night visits.

Angleton gave little away about his career, but he did reveal to us a rather fascinating episode involving Mary Meyer, the wife of Cord Meyer, one of his colleagues and once CIA station chief in London. Mary, who had been one of President Kennedy's many mistresses, was mysteriously found shot dead on the towpath of the Georgetown Canal the year after Kennedy's assassination, and her killer was never found. Angleton, whose wife Cicely was a close friend of Mary Meyer's, immediately went round and searched Mary Meyer's house and eventually found her diary, taking it as 'A matter of national security,' he told us. As far as I know the diary has never been seen since, and it was only years later that that particular Kennedy affair became known.

Angleton was not only head of counter-intelligence, but also ran the CIA's Israeli desk. He had the closest of links with the Israeli intelligence services and his pro-Israeli feelings made him almost as deeply suspicious of the Arabs as he was of the Soviet Union. The most extreme example of his anti-communist obsession was the bizarre conviction he frequently expressed to me that the split between the two communist superpowers, the Soviet Union and China, was all a cunning disinformation plot to fool the West.

Jim was, however, a kindly and charming friend whose chief interests outside the Cold War were fly-fishing and growing orchids. Just before we left for Moscow he lent us, for a holiday, his palatial fishing lodge on the Brule River in Wisconsin where Philby had once been a guest.

When I met Kim in Moscow shortly afterwards, I mentioned that we had spent our final days in the States in Angleton's lodge. 'Oh really, I remember it well,' said Kim. 'How's Jim? Does he still make his own flies?'

10

Moscow

Persecution

'Orlov, Orlov, Orlov,' roared a crowd of dissidents outside a Soviet People's Court as they spotted the diminutive figure of Yuri Orlov. 'Courage!' shouted Andrei Sakharov as Orlov, his fellow human-rights champion, was bundled into a windowless police van after being sentenced to imprisonment in Siberia.

For four days the dissidents, the foreign press and a diplomat from the American Embassy clutching a bag of sandwiches and a bottle of mineral water, had kept vigil outside the court as the trial of Orlov – a physicist and founder member of the Moscow Helsinki human rights monitoring group – proceeded. We approached the entrance to the empty court building each day to be told that the courtroom was not yet open. Then, as if by magic, the court was packed by a KGB 'rent-a-crowd', spirited in from the back, and we were told that every seat was taken.

Suddenly the trial was over. Jostled and pushed by KGB thugs, Professor Sakharov, his tall, bald-headed figure dominating the scene, berated the sullen crowd emerging from the court who refused to reveal Orlov's sentence – 12 years' hard labour. However, it was the appearance of tiny Irina Orlov, clutching a bunch of spring flowers and still managing to smile, that transformed the scene outside the court. She showed no sign of self-pity, and her appearance at that moment seemed to uplift her supporters, as if it was she who was comforting them.

I had arrived in Moscow in August 1977, at the height of Leonid Brezhnev's neo-Stalinist purge of the dissidents and was now seeing it in action. Brezhnev had made international agreements to respect human rights, but he had no intention of complying with them.

137

Instead, the KGB were now engaged in eliminating the courageous group of dissidents, headed by Sakharov, who were telling the world about political repression and conditions in the *gulag*, and the psychiatric wards.

Most of the crowd outside the court were eventually picked off one by one and sentenced for crimes against the state, while Sakharov was exiled to Gorky – one of the many areas of the Soviet Union forbidden to foreigners and out of reach of the press.

Amidst the flurry of activity outside the court that day, we managed to pile Irina Orlov into a car and drove her back to our press compound. We were pursued at high speed by a Volga carload of leather-jacketed KGB who bumped us and tried to force us off the road. A Reuters correspondent driving our car gave them the slip by turning onto an overpass at the very last second, too late for our pursuers to follow.

The Orlovs typified the incredible courage of a small group of Russians prepared to sacrifice everything in a seemingly hopeless struggle against a monstrous state. The vast majority of Russians, with a history of repression from Tsars to Commissars, had a built-in instinct to keep their heads down and hated the dissidents for stirring up trouble which could bring about further repression.

The Orlov's apartment was in a comparatively prosperous Moscow suburb nicknamed by correspondents 'dissident hill' where scientists and university people lived and where they kept open house for human-rights campaigners. Irina, an art historian, only became a dissident as a result of her husband's persecution. A feature of their flat, ironically, was a large portrait of Kafka, whose nightmares had now become their reality.

Chatting outside the courthouse at the Orlov trial, one of the dissidents told me that years ago during the Stalin days he had decided to keep cuttings of articles, in order to show his son when he was grown up how things really had been. 'But today', he said 'my son has grown up and he does not need these articles for he can see how things are for himself.' But as Irina came out of the court his mood seemed to brighten. 'How can someone who looks so small and frail have so much spirit?' he asked.

The Years of Stagnation

Arriving in Moscow for the first time, I had the curious impression that the Bolsheviks had seized power not decades ago, but just the day before yesterday – and that the year was 1917. It was a time warp.

Everywhere were the slogans 'Glory to the Communist Party of the Soviet Union', the huge, heroic social realism posters portraying soldiers, peasants and workers, the sinister Tatar features of Lenin – and the drabness of the people and the buildings of an immediately post-revolutionary society.

Nor had there been any change in the ethos of the regime from the days when a small, ruthless minority had seized power and which still ruled through secretiveness and terror – as if a counter-revolution was a threat just down the road. Once, watching a huge October Revolution parade of tanks and guns in Red Square, I glanced through an open door of a Kremlin tower at the entrance to the square and saw it packed with heavily armed special forces in battle fatigues. Clearly even on October Revolution Day no one was to be trusted, not even the Soviet forces parading past President Brezhnev.

Although by the late 1970s there was a general feeling of disillusionment over the failure of the communist system, its founder Lenin was still viewed as a sort of god. Thousands from all over the Soviet Union would queue up in Red Square every day to see his shrivelled corpse which was withdrawn every year for a *remont* (a repair job) – a new ear, and sometimes a new nose.

It was Lenin who set the path for Russia's disastrous 70 years of communism. Stalin, finally reviled by Nikita Khrushchev in his 'secret speech' to the All Union Congress in 1956, was no aberration. His secret police state, concentration camps and massacre of peasants, clergy and intellectuals were an inevitable extension of the evil system that Lenin had put in place. However, the unprecedented scale of Stalin's repression and brutality set its stamp on the minds of the Soviet people and even today – generations after his death – it remains a permanent fixture in their national psyche.

Just days before the invasion of Afghanistan, I visited Stalin's birthplace at Gori in Georgia for the hundredth anniversary of his birth. There was a thirty-foot statue of Josef Stalin, the man whom the Soviet Union has acknowledged was responsible for the deaths of 'no fewer than 20 million' of its citizens. To many Georgians, however, he remains the local boy who made good – the great wartime leader who built the nation into a superpower. To the ageing Brezhnev leadership in the Kremlin who had inherited his tyrannical system of government, Stalin was an embarrassment and a problem too big to go away.

The spirit of Stalin remained as an ever-present monster lurking in the Kremlin, ready to be unleashed against any opposition to the more liberal governments that succeeded the dictator. Stalin's secret police still survived and to maintain the unspoken threat of a return to the old repression, Brezhnev ended the de-Stalinisation policy of Nikita Khrushchev and began to accentuate Stalin's 'positive side'. The surviving leaders in the Kremlin never forgave Khrushchev for his 'secret speech' to the All Union Congress, but how to explain away the fact that the leadership of the Soviet Union for almost half its lifetime had fallen into the hands of the biggest mass murderer in history was no simple task.

It had to be a very slow process without risking new outrage among the communist parties in Eastern Europe and the West. But the Kremlin officials were past masters at rewriting history, and by the late 1970s, no reference to the Stalin purges could be found in school textbooks. Even the 1976 Soviet Encyclopaedia's reference to Stalin's 'miscalculations' at the outbreak of the Second World War – a euphemism for his slaughter of half the Red Army officer corps before the Nazi invasion – was omitted from later issues.

The official Soviet Diary for 1979 also let Stalin off lightly. It described him as 'a prominent figure of the Communist party of the Soviet Union'. No reference here to the millions of peasants deported in cattle trucks to Siberia, or the terrible famine and cannibalism that followed his agricultural policy.

In Gori you can still see the little wooden house where Josef Djugashvili, later called Stalin, the son of a cobbler, was born. Expelled from a theological seminary in Tbilisi he became a marxist, joined Lenin and after the latter's death, succeeded him.

In the 1930s Stalin, with his evil secret police chief Lavrenty Beria at his side, became a psychotic killer, obsessed with treason and conspiracy, as millions perished in the purges and show trials. When the Germans invaded in 1941, Stalin appeared to go into a state of shock and hysteria; but soon rallied and became the competent, ruthless war leader who not only defeated the enemy, but established the Soviet empire in Eastern Europe.

During my time in the Soviet Union it was almost impossible to meet anyone whose family or close friends had not been touched by imprisonment or death as a result of the Stalin terror. My translator Nelly still remembered, as a little girl, with cold fear, warnings about Beria cruising around Moscow in his limousine, picking up school-girls who were never seen again. The Soviet leaders were so scared of Beria that, after Stalin's death, Khrushchev carried a gun to protect himself when Beria was arrested at pistol point at a Kremlin meeting.

But Stalin still has his fans, and not only in Georgia, who look back to 'the good old days' when vodka and caviar were cheap and the Soviet Union was a superpower feared by the Western world. On my visit to Georgia, however, there were some who still remembered Stalin with fear and hatred and lowered their voices when they spoke of the terror. Stalin was no less ruthless in Georgia than in the rest of the Soviet Union and Georgians suffered as much as any others from Stalin's paranoia.

Nevertheless, most Georgians remain proud of their notorious son. 'When we toast here we first drink to the family, second to Stalin and third to Georgia' said one Stalin admirer as he staggered over to our table in a Tbilisi restaurant clutching a bottle of local 'champanski' sparkling wine. 'To Stalin, Roosevelt and Churchill' said another adding 'We don't find leaders like that today'.

The problem with Stalin and why he still haunts post-communist Russia is that he fits so neatly into the nation's historical tradition – Stalin was a natural, historic successor to those Tsars who merely lacked the technological resources to massacre Russians on the same scale. The KGB was a direct successor to the Tsarist secret police, and centuries of repression have understandably given the Russian people a built-in fear of authority which provides a conducive climate for any leader seeking to impose dictatorship.

At the same time the Russians, whose entire history has been one of foreign invasions, constantly feel under threat and possess an instinctive need for a strong leader – even if he should turn out to be another Ivan the Terrible or another Joseph Stalin. It would, perhaps, be wise for the West to take more note of the likely consequences of this Russian characteristic while blithely planning to extend the NATO alliance right up against the Russian borders. The emergence of a new Stalin is an ever-present threat to a great nation sunk in economic misery which perceives the enemy at its frontiers.

Khrushchev considerably modified Stalin's reign of terror, but the Communist Party continued to dominate all aspects of Soviet life and new waves of oppression were launched against dissidents and the church. But Khrushchev's growing personality cult, his flamboyant peasant style which shocked ordinary, conservative Russians, and his unpredictability which nearly caused world nuclear war, led to his replacement by the grey men of the Kremlin.

Improbably, Leonid Brezhnev, a vain, greedy and limited man, rose to the top of the heap and gave the Soviet Union what became known as 'the years of stagnation'. However, as living conditions worsened and corruption grew, Brezhnev also presided over a vast arms build-up which put Moscow ahead of Washington in some key areas of nuclear armaments. By embarking in the late 1970s on the

installation of a new generation of medium-range nuclear missiles
targeted on Western Europe, Brezhnev sparked an East–West arms
race that left the Soviets spending a crippling 30 per cent of GNP on
defence. His impetuous invasion of Afghanistan in 1979 was the final
disaster of the Brezhnev era – and led directly to the collapse of the
Soviet empire.

It is alarming how quickly you adjust to life in a corrupt and stag-
nating dictatorship, a secretive society where all knowledge can be
dangerous and where surveillance is in the air you breathe. But however much one has read and heard of the Soviet Union, it fails to
prepare you for the breathtaking cynicism, hypocrisy and corruption in a country which has superpower status and the standards of a
seedy Third World republic. 'I am privileged!' shouts a sturdy woman
charging to the front of a shopping queue. And no one dares to
challenge her.

With most of the nation's wealth diverted to the military and security establishments, there was a permanent scramble among the
privileged for what was left over – headed by the top members of the
Communist Party.

For members and the families of the Politburo, the Central
Committee, senior ranks of the military and the KGB, there were
exclusive foreign currency shops for clothes, food and drink, hospital clinics, a cardiac centre, hairdressers, beauticians and even a
cosmetic surgery unit. Opposite where I once lived there was a top
people's tailor's shop – a small shopfront with curtains permanently
drawn outside which Zil limousines would park while servants
brought in suits and dresses for alteration.

Foreign correspondents, like diplomats and Western businessmen,
also lived highly privileged lives – but we had to pay for it in our own
hard currency. In return for sterling we purchased coupons to be
used in hard currency shops providing imported goods, and these
coupons naturally became much desired by the Russians. despite it
being a criminal offence for Soviet citizens to hold hard currency or
coupons, or for foreigners to give it to them. But translators, drivers
or secretaries would not work for you without hard currency bribes,
so you immediately became sucked into an illegal system which made
you vulnerable to criminal prosecution.

One of the most corrupt of the government departments was the
Diplomatic Corps Service Bureau, (UPDK) which dealt with the
needs of foreign residents. Controlled by the KGB, it handled travel
arrangements and hotel reservations, and provided all local employ-
ees and all accommodation, both office and domestic. It was, of

course, a major source of intelligence information since all local staff, embassy chauffeurs, chambermaids, office cleaners, plumbers and electricians were forced to spy on their employers and report regularly to their control. One British ambassador was seduced by an embassy maid and had to be recalled.

Early on, we saw a striking example of the all-embracing nature of this surveillance when a maid signalled to us to come into our bathroom and then turned the taps full on before she began a whispered conversation about wanting to work for us. A top flat in the foreigner's block where we eventually lived was occupied by the KGB as the surveillance centre where recordings from all the apartments were made and tapes regularly changed.

Arriving with the distinct disadvantage of having no flat or office, I was obliged to throw myself on the doubtful mercy of the UPDK as the only legal source of accommodation, armed only with the *Telegraph*'s assurance that we could leave Moscow after six months if nothing came up. The issue of our accommodation was even taken up by our Foreign Secretary, David Owen, who came over for talks with the Soviet government shortly after my arrival. I was briefed about his discussions by the Minister at the British Embassy, Robert Wade-Gery. He felt the matter sufficiently confidential to take me into the embassy's supposedly bug-free top security room where he switched on a scrambler. It made a background sound like a very noisy cocktail party – which may have fooled the Russians but certainly confused me. In the meantime, we led a nomadic life camping out in flats of colleagues while they were on leave and who lent me their office facilities.

During our homeless period a CBS correspondent, also trying to set up in Moscow, had better fortune than us. He discovered that the then director of the UPDK had previously been a Soviet ambassador to the UN and that in the United States had developed a passion for golf. This naturally presented him with a problem when he returned to Moscow since there was not a single golf course in the whole of the Soviet Union. In a brilliant stroke, the CBS man had flown in from the States the very latest electronic golf machine for indoor golf which was set up on the carpet of the director's office. Within days the CBS was provided with a splendid apartment overlooking the Moskva river.

Meeting at the Bolshoi

I was unable to come up with an idea to match the indoor golf-machine and our six months were almost over when our fortunes changed. On a snowy February night in 1978 when we went to the Bolshoi, Moyra spotted across the stalls my old colleague Kim Philby with his pretty Russian wife Rufina. Kim had gone to ground and had rarely been sighted since his defection in 1963. Unlike his fellow spies Guy Burgess and Donald Maclean, it was clear the KGB was keeping him under wraps and no one knew his address.

'As I live and breathe, Dick Beeston!' Kim said in his old familiar voice, with a broad smile, as I tapped him on the shoulder during an interval of the opera 'Otello'. 'And Moyra. I heard you were in Moscow. I hope the Soviet authorities are looking after you well.' He then introduced us to his wife Rufina who was smartly dressed in a black top and velvet skirt. She looked about 20 years younger than Kim, who was then 65.

It was an odd experience to meet an old friend, who seemed little changed, after so much had happened in the intervening years, and who had become so notorious. Naively, perhaps, I had never really believed Kim to be a Soviet agent until his defection to Moscow. Since my arrival, I had often wondered how I would feel, and how I should react if I ran into him. Any moral dilemma, I must admit, was however easily resolved by that fact that I was a newspaper correspondent in Moscow and this was a fascinating story.

Kim, after so little contact with his past, was clearly delighted to see us – particularly since the encounter was pure chance and should not arouse suspicion with his KGB handlers. He chatted about the past, remembered the names of our children, who had been at school with his in Beirut, and was interested to hear that my son was at his old school, Westminster. 'Ah Westminster. You should be careful, sometimes they produce some, some . . .' he began to stutter. 'Bad hats' I suggested – and he grinned.

His stutter was still apparent, but not the excruciating speech impediment he had displayed during his last, heavy-drinking days in Beirut when we were neighbours of him and his late wife Eleanor. 'How do you think he looks?' Rufina asked me, in a very wifely way, when told how long it was since we last met. 'Older but fitter than when I last saw him' I replied. 'I don't drink so much as when I was in Beirut,' said Kim.

'How are you finding things in Moscow?' he enquired. At this, I complained about my lack of accommodation and the probability that I would have to return to Washington if I could not find somewhere to live. 'Actually,' he said 'I'm leaving for a bit soon. But', he added with his special disarming smile, 'It wouldn't do to have you staying in my place and rifling around with my papers!' However, when I saw him again in the second interval of the opera he told me he had been thinking about my problems. 'I still know one or two people and I'll see what I can do' he promised.

Two days later UPDK called me and asked me to go round and look at a – by Soviet standards – rather elegant flat below the Reuters bureau. I had already been negotiating with them about the flat but had recently been told it had been allocated to the Jamaican ambassador. 'What's the point – you have already given it to someone else,' I pointed out. 'No, no,' came the reply. 'Go and see it, and if you want it, it's yours.'

Later, we had a letter from Kim which said 'I am glad you got your flat at last, and would like to think it was the result of a few telephone calls I made after our meeting at the Bolshoi. One of the callees made surprisingly encouraging noises. But then again it may have been a coincidence.' He added 'Did I really say "As I live and breathe?" I have tried it out several times and it sounds unlike me. It was more probably "Good God" – and you, with your usual tact, altered the phrase for fear that my invocation of the Almighty might get me into trouble with the authorities.'

At the end of the opera, I had dashed round to the UPI office to file the story for the *Telegraph*'s first editions, and in a strange way to get it out of my system. It was the everydayness of the encounter which I found so odd. Just two old colleagues meeting by chance after years, as if nothing had happened to a friendship except the passage of time, when in fact so much had happened and nothing could be the same again.

All three of the gentlemen spies, Philby, Burgess and Maclean are now long dead, having done incalculable harm to their country. Of the three, Kim appeared to have suffered the least, wearing his treason like a comfortable old tweed suit. The Philby I met in Moscow had the same English charm and ease of manner that so successfully fooled the British intelligence service and the CIA – and his friends and colleagues.

People whom he had betrayed longed to hear reports of his suffering and loneliness, with only a bottle of vodka for comfort, in the alien twilight world of Moscow exiles. Shortly after his defection Kim had betrayed his American wife Eleanor, who had given up everything for him, and whose place had been taken briefly by Maclean's wife Melissa. But by the time we met him, he appeared to be finally content with his young and affectionate Russian wife Rufina.

As usual he gave nothing away. However when Moyra mentioned some of the problems I was having with the Soviet authorities, Kim asked 'But Moyra, how long has Dick been here?' 'Six months' she replied. 'Moyra,' said Kim looking her straight in the eyes, 'I have been here sixteen years.'

After our encounter we wrote to Kim through his post box suggesting another meeting, but he turned us down. Years later, after the collapse of the Soviet Union, we were finally invited to the Philby flat by his widow. Rufina told us that Kim had wanted to see us again but had not been permitted to do so. Perhaps the KGB too was not certain about his loyalties.

When we were stationed in Moscow, Kim's residence was a well-kept secret. It turned out to be right in the centre of town near Pushkin square – an old-fashioned and by Russian standards spacious apartment, full of mementos and 1950s furniture.

It was in 1994 – 16 years after our Bolshoi encounter that we went to dine with Rufina, while I was staying in Moscow with my son Richard – *The Times* Bureau chief there. Although Kim had died several years before, she left no doubt that she was still very much in love with him. That boyish charm that I had seen work so successfully on his other wives and friends had had the same success with his last wife, apparently prepared to forgive his horrific drinking bouts and his history of deceits and betrayals. 'I had the most wonderful 18 years of my life with Kim,' she said. And somehow you believe her.

She had kept Kim Philby's presence uncannily alive and it was easy to imagine him sitting in the next room, typing at his desk where there was a photograph of him as a pipe-smoking Cambridge undergraduate. There was also an old photo of the Normandie Hotel in Beirut where we used to meet for drinks when we were both working for British newspapers.

Over a dinner of zakuski, sturgeon, vodka and Georgian wine, Rufina told us how she first met Kim on a blind date in 1970 with George Blake. One can only wonder if Blake and Philby ever discussed who should take credit for doing the most damage to Britain and the West by their betrayals!

On the date when Rufina first met Kim, at the American Ballet on Ice, she was a stunning young woman. She had no English and Kim had only very basic Russian. But he said to her in Russian 'Please take off your glasses, I would like to see your eyes.' Later he told her that he had decided within seconds to marry her.

When we met Rufina, she was still an attractive, intelligent woman in her late fifties, whose pension as a widow of a senior KGB officer had almost disappeared in post-communist inflation. To make ends meet she had had to sell off some of her husband's books, letters and personal belongings, but still on the wall was an Italian engraving of Rome – a present from Kim's friend Anthony Blunt.

Before leaving, I asked her if she remembered Kim's efforts to find us somewhere to live in Moscow and our allocation of an apartment shortly after our meeting with them. 'Oh yes,' she said. 'Kim was so happy. He said it is not often you are able to do things to help old friends.'

A Spiked Drink

There was naturally no love lost between the resident Western foreign correspondent and the Soviet authorities. The whole basis for the relationship was that of reciprocity, which meant that if I was expelled, the KGB would lose a valuable spy in London working for the Soviet media. This gave us reasonable security except of course against tit-for-tat expulsions – such as times when the British government threw out a bunch of Russian agents. At the same time, the Soviet authorities were not too worried about what appeared in British newspapers, since Soviet citizens had no access to them and the only one on sale was the communist *Morning Star*.

By the time I arrived in Moscow the authorities had even given up direct censorship and I had a telex machine in my flat through which I filed straight to London. This more relaxed attitude to the capitalist press did not of course preclude KGB attempts at harassment, blackmail and round-the-clock surveillance which all seemed a bit of a joke at the start. But over the years it takes a toll on your nerves. Although you quickly become accustomed to living in a police state, you don't realise the build-up of pressure until, when flying out of Moscow, you feel a huge weight lifting from your shoulders.

The atmosphere of surveillance was all-embracing. Brezhnev's Russia was just about as near as you could get to living in George Orwell's *Nineteen Eighty-Four*. Incidentally, *Nineteen Eighty-Four* and *Animal Farm* were – a tribute to the author – at the very top of the Kremlin's banned booklist. They were the only two titles forbidden to appear at the Moscow International Book Fair of 1977, which was the first of its kind and supposed to be censorship free.

To make surveillance easier for the KGB, every foreigner's car had a number plate which enabled the *militsia* to recognise instantly your nationality, your profession and you by your own personal number. If your plate started with 'D' you were a diplomat, or 'K' a correspondent. The next number indicated your country – 01 for Britain, 04 for the United States. You were only allowed to drive

12 miles out of town without permission and police were posted at that distance on all roads leaving Moscow. If, for example, you obtained permission from the UPDK to drive to the cathedral at Zagorsk – about 30 miles out of town – you were not permitted to stop even to picnic by the roadside. To take a train to another Soviet city (provided it was not in a zone forbidden to foreigners) you had to obtain your travel ticket from the UPDK, who would also book your train carriage and your hotel. This would enable the KGB to bug your train compartment and your hotel room and to alert everyone of your travel plans.

Before leaving for Moscow, Moyra went to see the recently separated wife of the *New York Times* Moscow correspondent for tips on life there. 'All I can say,' she informed Moyra, 'is that if your marriage is at all threadbare, Moscow will destroy it.'

In the enclosed world of a foreigners' compound, guarded day and night at the entrance to the courtyard by the *militsia*, life was cosy but suffocating. Protected from the big, bad world outside, there was no need to lock your front door. The only possible intruders could be the KGB and they had the key! The system certainly had advantages and many foreigners living today in the lawless city that Moscow has become would happily trade their lot for the security of KGB surveillance. On a recent visit to Russia I had hardly set foot in St Petersburg before I was mugged. This would never have happened in the old days with the protective presence of a KGB tail.

The sense of isolation was increased by the difficulty of getting to know ordinary Russians, apart from authorised contacts or dissidents who had already burned their boats and were mostly waiting for exit visas.

There was a 'twilight zone' of rather sad Western expatriates who, either through early and misplaced enthusiasm for the communist system or romantic involvement with Russians, were permanently stuck behind the Iron Curtain. Most of them, usually ex-diplomats or journalists working for Soviet publishing houses were thoroughly disillusioned by the system but had nowhere else to go.

We used to meet them at the flat of Terry Bushell the cockney correspondent of the *Morning Star*. The son of a Deptford dustman, Terry started out as a sports correspondent and became a communist in response to the social inequalities in Britain. Terry was charming, politically naive and deeply shocked to find the Soviet system contained far worse inequalities than the capitalist West. He married Lara, a beautiful, lively Russian whose knowledge of English literature put us all to shame. They had a baby boy called Pickwick, and after they went to live in England Terry wrote a book called *Marriage of Inconvenience* which gave an illuminating view of life in Moscow.

Apart from the twilight people, who included Robert Dalgleish, a former British diplomat who had sacrificed his career by marrying a Russian at the height of the Cold War, we had the rare opportunity of meeting Russians at the Bushell's flat. Most of them were Lara's relations and friends, and for the first time Moyra and I saw the contrast between the official, glum face of Muscovites in the street and their warmth and fun when they were behind closed doors and having a party.

Another unusual expatriate character we got to know was Len Wincott, an ex-Royal Naval rating who was sent to prison in the 1930s for being a ringleader in the Invergordon naval mutiny, caused by a cut in seamen's wages. Outraged by his treatment, he promptly joined the Communist Party and unwisely decided to live in the Soviet Union. Paradoxically, he remained devoted to the Royal Navy and his personal hero was Lord Louis Mountbatten! This almost got him into trouble. When he was eventually invited to a Queen's birthday party at the Embassy he found a signed photograph of Mountbatten irresistible, slipped it in his pocket but finally returned it.

We visited Len, a small, balding man in his seventies who had retained his Midlands accent, and his much younger Russian wife Elena. They lived in the midst of nowhere – a desolate Moscow suburb with footpaths criss-crossing the mud of abandoned building sites in an apartment block that looked like English council flats of the 1950s. Len, to Elena's discomfort, spoke scornfully about the Soviet system and the KGB, and seemed unconcerned about the bugs doubtless installed in his flat. He had been ill served by his devotion to the communist cause and was bitter about the late Harry Pollitt, former head of the British Communist party.

It was Pollitt who advised him to go to Moscow. And it was Pollitt who told him to allow his British passport to expire and become a Soviet citizen. Len survived the dreadful 900-day siege of Leningrad only to fall victim to Stalin's purges after the war. Without ever learning what the charges were he spent ten years in a *gulag* near the Arctic Circle and was released after Stalin's death to be told that his sentence had been a judicial error. The camp had been run largely by criminal convict thugs. Len lived through it, he told us, because of how he had learned to look after himself as a boy in the Royal Navy! 'After that experience,' he told us 'you can survive anything'.

Shortly after we left Moscow, Len managed to fulfil the dream of his old age. Sponsored by a British newspaper he took Elena to

London on her first visit, rented a huge limousine and showed her
the House of Commons, St Paul's Cathedral and Buckingham Palace.

One of the best places to meet the local Russians without compromising them was stark naked in the old 'Sadunovsky Banya' – the
bath-house built in tsarist days, where you beat each other with birch
branches and, against the rules, drank vodka, smoked and ate fishy
snacks in the changing rooms. But to follow up an unauthorised
acquaintance with a Soviet citizen could easily jeopardise his career
and his whole life – and quite probably force him to inform on you to
the KGB.

One youngish Russian I met told me a tragic story of how his life
was doomed by a chance encounter, when he was a student, with an
American family at a Moscow railway station. Offering to carry one of
their bags, he became friendly with them during their visit and with
their daughter, a musician, about his own age.

For some years after this they kept up a correspondence until one
day he was summoned by the KGB. They had learned that an
American orchestra was visiting Moscow and that the girl was one of
the musicians. The KGB agent made it clear that he had read all the
letters that had passed between the two and that he wanted the
Russian to meet the girl when she arrived and spy on the orchestra
throughout its tour. He refused and shortly afterwards was thrown
out of his engineering job, placed on the KGB blacklist and was
unable to get any other employment. In desperation, he tried to stow
away aboard a ship leaving Leningrad but was caught and sent to
prison. Out of gaol he phoned up to arrange a meeting with myself
and a colleague. When we met him he told us his story, but that was
the first and last time we saw him.

Perhaps the most tragic victim of the system was a distressed, tooth-
less woman in her fifties who looked more like seventy. A sort of
Ancient Mariner, she haunted foreign newspaper bureaux to tell her
story and plead for help. As a beautiful young girl translating for the
British Embassy during the war she had fallen in love and married a
British naval attaché but was refused permission to accompany him
when he was posted back to Britain.

He left aboard a warship from Murmansk. In desperation, she disguised herself as a sailor but was picked up by the KGB as she tried to
board the ship. Years of incarceration in a prison camp followed,
leaving her fearful and unhinged. When she told me her story she
would break off every few moments and point to the ceiling light –
the warning everyone used to indicate they were being bugged. She
would then frantically write something on a piece of paper in front of

her which I took to be information she did not want to be recorded. But when eventually I looked at the piece of paper at the end of the interview all that was written on it was 'KGB, KGB, KGB', covering the page.

Another horror story was told to me by Fitzroy Maclean, during a visit to Moscow, going back to the days when he was a diplomat in Moscow in 1938 at the time of the pre-war purges. He met a beautiful young ballet dancer at a diplomatic cocktail party and took her out to the cinema next day. He heard no more from her but some days later her mother phoned him to say that her daughter had disappeared and that she would never forgive him.

Although such stories are in the past, the ghetto life for foreigners in the 1970s continued to provide an isolated and unreal existence, surrounded by official hostility. It reminded one of a rather bad English boarding school and made for a uniquely close relationship within the foreign community and within your own particular ghetto block. We all gave lots of parties to cheer each other up through the long winter months. In this overheated atmosphere the inevitable affairs were conducted with little chance of privacy. Diplomats were supposed to report sexual relationships, even with members of the foreign communities, to their ambassadors so that the chances of KGB blackmail could be assessed. Any sexual relations with Soviet citizens normally led to immediate postings.

The extra-marital life of the foreign community must at least have added some spice to the unfortunate KGB agents who would have to endure hours of boring bedroom conversations between married couples – until a stranger arrived on the scene! The most dangerous relationship, from the blackmail point of view, was homosexuality – still a crime in the Soviet Union and punishable by five years in prison.

One unfortunate diplomat came up against Soviet law before my arrival. He contracted a venereal disease and, too embarrassed to see the British embassy doctor, went to a Soviet physician. Shortly afterwards, a policeman arrived at the embassy with an order for the diplomat to attend a court to testify, under Soviet law, about his sexual partners. After this the diplomat dared not leave the embassy compound for fear of arrest and remained a prisoner until a deal was finally done with the Soviet authorities to smuggle him out of the country.

Our compound was a grim apartment block, but less shoddy than most since it had been built not by Russians but by German POWs just after the war. It looked on to the Sadova road that encircled

Moscow. A good deal of the traffic was made up of empty trucks driving round the Sadova ring, building up mileage to qualify for their monthly petrol ration.

The liveliest people in our building, and good for morale, were a group of young British defence attachés whose job was to spy on the Soviet military and try not to get caught. They travelled almost incessantly around the Soviet Union gathering information on defence establishments, troop movements and new Soviet military equipment. Their wives were encouraged to travel with them to reduce the chances of entrapment and, with their husbands, were frequently roughed up and arrested.

Although there is obviously a limit to the amount of military intelligence to be obtained through a pair of binoculars or a conversation in a restaurant, such activity is a useful adjunct to other forms of intelligence such as spy satellites and undercover agents. It can also be used to confuse the enemy, leading him to suspect the work of a military attaché when the real source is perhaps a spy in his own midst.

In one incident while we were in Moscow, two British officers and their wives were seized by a group of so-called 'concerned citizens' who roughed them up and arrested them. They were searched, had their diplomatic passports confiscated and were interrogated for hours without being allowed to contact their embassy.

One gung-ho naval attaché broke his leg one night when he slipped on ice in Leningrad while spying on a shipyard where a Soviet aircraft carrier was under construction. In this case, improbably, KGB agents who were tailing him helped to get him to hospital!

There were frequent cases of then-defence attachés being drugged and then waking up to find themselves being photographed naked in bed with a woman or sometimes a man. Some American attachés even resorted to carrying their own food and drink on their trips.

Although it was one of the trickiest jobs in peacetime service – and the only one in which servicemen actually came face to face with 'the enemy' – it was poorly rewarded by the British armed forces. Instead, when these attachés returned to their ship or regiments, they usually found that they had lost promotion prospects and that their careers had badly slipped. One young submariner we knew in Moscow was unable to find a suitable posting when he returned and reluctantly resigned from the navy. Other assistant defence attachés with the equivalent rank of major had to take postings that they normally would have been offered three or four years earlier in their careers.

After some research I discovered that American attachés in Moscow received good postings and promotions, often taking on high-level intelligence jobs at the end of their assignments. They were given exhaustive debriefings and would then make lecture tours of military establishments to give an eye-witness view of the Soviet military establishment. But British officers returning from Moscow usually found little interest taken in the knowledge they had with great difficulty obtained, and on the strength of this I wrote a piece for the *Telegraph* headed 'Attachés in Russia Brave Harassment With No Reward'. It was satisfying to learn that the issue was raised in Parliament, came to the attention of Margaret Thatcher and that, apparently, returning attachés were given a better deal.

We in the Western press were also targets for Soviet dirty tricks. For small offences our tyres would be slashed or car windows broken by 'hooligans', somehow invisible to the ever-present *militsia*. The *Financial Times* correspondent David Satter, whose family were Jewish Ukrainians and who had good contacts with dissident Jews – had an especially hard time with his car and office being broken into.

However, the worst treatment while we were in Moscow was reserved for Robin Knight, the British correspondent of *US News and World Report*. The Soviet authorities, who liked to keep their enemies in compartments, had a particular dislike for an Englishman representing an American publication. Robin made himself even more unpopular by producing well-researched articles about the desperate state of the Soviet economy, which were frequently broadcast back to the Soviet Union in Russian by American radio stations.

He became a frequent target for attack in the Soviet press and towards the end of his assignment decided to go with his wife Jean on a final visit to Soviet Central Asia. While in Tashkent, Robin took on an Intourist guide, whom, he noted, was not very well informed about his subject, and after a morning's sightseeing the guide implored the Knights to attend his birthday party at a teahouse in the town. They wanted to return to their hotel, but out of politeness agreed.

The party was crowded but Jean noticed that, after Robin had had one drink, he had suddenly disappeared and the nightmare began. When she asked where her husband had gone, Jean suddenly found herself surrounded by men saying 'don't worry, you stay with us, he has probably had too much to drink'.

She fought her way out to find Robin looking like death and vomiting in the gutter. She stayed with him, noting the birthday party had suddenly evaporated, and finally got him into a taxi. When she arrived at the hotel she found the door locked against her but it was at last opened by a tourist inside. By this time Robin was practically unconscious and as she dragged him into the hallway a policeman came forward and tried to seize him.

When she asked him what he was doing, he replied 'your husband is drunk, I'm taking him to the police station'. When he came forward Jean, a slight, slim, woman flew at him, then dragged Robin into the lift and got him to the bedroom. There she put him in a hot bath; his teeth were chattering so badly that she had to put a handkerchief in his mouth.

By luck, she managed to get a call through to the American ambassador in Moscow, who said they were flying down a member of the embassy to collect him and that she was to keep the bedroom door locked until he arrived. Robin recovered fully, but could easily have died from what was clearly a massive drug overdose slipped to him by an obviously over-zealous KGB agent in Tashkent who spiked his drink.

'By chance', a passing photographer happened to film Robin being sick in the street in Tashkent and a Moscow newspaper ran the story with a caption stating that he was a typical drunken member of the Western press.

The Knight affair was an extreme example of the malevolence of the Soviet system and of the dangerous results of allowing the KGB to run out of control. It was given headline treatment in the American press and a goodwill visit to Moscow by a group of American congressmen at that time ended as a public relations disaster for the Russians.

Secret Society

Despite all the ideological propaganda trimmings of Soviet communism, there was little ideology left in the Soviet Union. What we were witnessing was a group of greedy old men hanging on to power and privilege as the economy atrophied. Their leader, Leonid Brezhnev, appeared little more than an effigy as I watched him shuffling down the steps of the Soviet embassy in Vienna supported by President Carter during the nuclear disarmament summit in 1979.

Brezhnev typified the Soviet leadership 60 years after the Bolshevik Revolution; with his hunting lodges and *dachas*, his fleet of foreign cars, his own literary prizes for his dishonest accounts of his role in the war – while the best writers were exiled – and his management of a society based on corruption and fear.

Life for the ordinary Muscovite, however, although grey and dismal, did still have its advantages. He faced none of the pressures of competition experienced by his contemporaries in the West, and provided that he kept his nose clean and played by the rules, he could be reasonably certain of a job, a crowded but warm apartment, enough food to eat, free education and a very basic health service. Absenteeism and alcoholism were an accepted way of life and rarely affected job security. 'We pretend to work, and they pretend to pay us' is how a typical Soviet worker would put it. There were few incentives for efficiency or dedication, and the work climate was ideal for the Russian layabout – of whom there were many. It was the Russian women, whether chipping ice from the pre-dawn streets, or running government departments, schools or hospital clinics, who seemed to hold things together.

Ambitious Russians worked hard for membership of the Communist Party, usually less from their belief in Leninist socialism than from a desire to enjoy some of the privileges of the ruling élite. Most of the luxuries of life for the under-privileged came through barter. A couple of tickets for the Bolshoi would ensure special attention from your local doctor, a bottle of vodka could purchase some caviar or oranges from the back door of a restaurant.

Viktor, the splendid driver we shared with UPI, who disdained Soviet authority and whose response to any request was 'no problem' always carried a few bottles of vodka with him in his car. He used them to bribe the traffic police, the customs and visa and airport officials. When our cat, Ming, was flown in from Washington, Viktor even talked his way into Moscow airport's control tower and spoke to the pilot to make sure Ming was on board.

However, despite the Soviet Union's secret and heavily censored society, it was not too hard to find out what was going on. Russians were expert at reading between the lines in their newspapers, avoiding the main story in *Pravda* about shoe or tractor production figures to find an obscure paragraph which, for example, might give a hint that things were not going all that well in the war in Afghanistan.

There was a fairly reliable, if sometimes highly coloured, grapevine of information about scandals in high places – such as Brezhnev's daughter's affair with the man who ran the Moscow circus and was also involved in diamond smuggling and the black market. Obtaining news from outside the Moscow ring road – including hundreds of thousands of square miles of territory permanently sealed off from the foreigner and secret cities whose very names were unknown – was more difficult. The foreign press therefore usually jumped at Foreign

Ministry tours of factories or other state enterprises in remote areas in case they saw something that was not on the itinerary or were able to speak to someone unauthorised, when their handlers were not looking.

On a visit to Murmansk, the press were split into groups and given the chance to spend an evening with a typical fisherman's family. The BBC man and I were taken to a tall, brand new apartment block and introduced to a smartly dressed fisherman's wife. Her husband, we were told, was away on a factory ship fishing off the coast of South America. Standing in as host was an elderly, gold-toothed, party hack who was wearing all his medals for the occasion.

Not only was the flat spotless and new, but all the cutlery, glasses and china had obviously just come out of a box. Our embarrassed hostess, who was supervising supper, had to keep asking where the glasses and plates and bottles were kept until it became obvious that she had arrived at the flat for the first time only just before us!

Vodka toasts to Anglo-Soviet friendship, the BBC and *The Daily Telegraph* were proposed at a fearsome rate and when we finally left for our hotel we saw a policeman, in a worse state than us, staggering ahead and eventually collapsing into a snowdrift. Outside our hotel the doors of the bar suddenly flung open and, like some arctic Western, a fighting mass of drunken Russians fell out, kicking and punching and staining the snow with blood. Passers-by seemed unsurprised, although some shouted that they should not behave like that in front of foreigners

At an interview laid on for us with the mayor of Murmansk, I asked him about the problems of alcoholism in his far northern city. There was no problem, he replied. Alcoholism was a bourgeois disease and did not occur in a socialist society.

At a puppet theatre we were taken to, I discovered that Winnie the Pooh – *Vinnie Pookh* – was a popular Russian favourite and his adventures with Christopher Robin and Piglet were being enacted by strange-looking, oversize Russian puppets. 'Who is this *Vinnie Pookh?*' a bewildered Eastern European correspondent on the trip asked me as Pooh sat on the stage with his pot of honey.

On a press visit to the great car factory at Togliatti on the Volga, where several Lada cars rolled off the production line every minute, we asked where the workers' car park was located. There isn't one, the factory manager told us. 'If this were an aircraft factory, would you expect every worker to own a plane?'

During our conducted tours we had not expected to find evidence of feudalism existing in the Soviet system. In Krasnodar, in the

Northern Caucasus, however, it appeared to be alive and well, in the figure of Hero of Socialist Labour Alexei Maistrenko, a bulky, formidable figure with two rows of gold teeth and the same earthy humour as Khrushchev. He was the general manager of a vast state rice-growing enterprise – one of the most successful in the Soviet Union – but he ran his estate more like a feudal landlord than a commissar. Most collective farms in the Soviet Union were disasters, and foreign correspondents were shown only the best. The Krasnodarsky State Farm was obviously a showpiece.

'A single principle reigns here,' said its boss. 'Those who work well receive material and moral remuneration for their efforts. Even milkmaids here get 250 roubles a month.' – a figure far above the national average. 'We look after our people and we are not taking on any outsiders.' His farm also provided university grants for its workers' children, a sports stadium, a playground, a large Ferris wheel, its own hospital and school of music.

A hostess in a full-length gown took us on a tour of the farm's art gallery and a room of satirical cartoons portraying inefficiency and corruption. We were then taken to a palatial ménage and were shown some magnificent thoroughbreds, including Arabs and Arabs crossed with Cossack breeds.

Back at the farm headquarters, where the all-mechanised rice farming activities were controlled by short-wave radio, our group drank a toast on Maistrenko's birthday. 'How old are you?' we asked. 'Seventy-five,' he replied – and crossed himself.

Maistrenko was obviously doing such a good job – or had friends in very high places – that he was allowed to run things his own way and seemed untroubled by the heavy hand of Soviet bureaucracy. The most incredible moment of the visit was when he showed off his horses with a display of dressage by a beautiful young woman in full riding habit.

His farm, he proudly announced, made its own *koumiss* – fermented mare's milk. 'One wife is not enough for those who drink *koumiss*' Maistrenko declared. The one question no one dared to ask our host was whether he exercised the feudal right of *droit de seigneur*. But in any case we were pretty sure we knew the answer.

There was not a great deal of contact between the British embassy, a splendid old sugar baron's mansion on the Moskva river, and the Russians. An ordinary Russian would be terrified to go near the place unless he had permission from the authorities. Those permitted to attend an embassy dinner usually experienced alarm – first on being confronted by the *militsia* at the gate and then on seeing a large oil painting on the staircase which looked exactly like Tsar Nicholas II. They had to be reassured that it was in fact King George V

One Anglo-Soviet event that did occur during our stay was held in Siberia. It was the 'British Week' at Novosibirsk. Some cynics called it Russia's revenge for a Soviet week in Hull or Wolverhampton! The high point of the occasion was a stunning British fashion show at a cavernous cinema. The local Siberians had never seen anything like it. All the fashions were off-the-peg, ready to wear, but looked fantastic on a group of Russian models brought in from Moscow.

Wearing the sort of clothes Russians had never seen before, and to sounds that they had never heard, the models strode across the stage to the music of 'Saturday Night Fever', as elegant on the catwalk as though they had left Paris the previous week. The girls would have loved to have bought the clothes, but the Russians insisted that they must all be packed up and sent back to England.

When I arrived at the cinema, the queue of Siberians hoping to see the show stretched through a snow-covered forest of silver birch and out of sight. Inside I noticed the first three rows of seats were empty until just minutes before the performance, when a crowd of middle-aged KGB and Party officials and their dowdy wives trooped in.

After the performance there was a question-and-answer programme chaired by Sir Fitzroy Maclean, the president of the GB–USSR association. Among the panel was the British minister Sir Robert Wade-Gery, and Moyra was picked to represent 'a typical British housewife', a choice which alarmed the Soviet organisers. The wife of a correspondent of a capitalist newspaper living in Moscow was clearly not to their liking and they said that she could not sit on the panel. Maclean and Wade-Gery stuck to their guns, stating it had been agreed in advance that a British housewife would sit on the panel to reply to 'free questions' from the audience and Moyra was their choice.

After a long delay, a compromise was reached and it was agreed that a Novosti newsagency man, Andrei Antonovsky, who had been sent from Moscow to keep an eye on things, should sit next to Moyra to correct any 'misunderstandings'. All the 'free questions' came from the first three rows. She was asked what was the main difference she found as a typical housewife between Britain and the Soviet Union. It was, she replied, lack of choice. The British were brought up to choose from alternatives. The Russians were never allowed choice. The answer went down like a lead balloon. Antonovsky then asked Moyra 'What do you mean by choice?' – which seemed to prove her point.

Another event was a school poetry-reciting competition, with the first prize a return air ticket to Britain. We all went to a Siberian school which prided itself on teaching English and heard the winner, a charming little Russian 12 year-old boy reciting from Robert Burns' 'My Heart is in the Highlands' with an almost authentic Scottish accent. Sadly, we heard later, he never did get his exit visa.

Fitzroy Maclean later took us on a brief sightseeing tour of the town. He was a keen photographer and demonstrated his success in managing to take pictures for his books in Russia, where every citizen is his own secret policeman. With a very small camera, a fairly long-range lens and a fast film, Fitzroy would shoot from the hip, unobserved, and claimed a high rate of success.

As part of his official duties, Fitzroy, who could drink anyone under the table, accepted an invitation to visit two Siberian vodka distilleries. One distillery would be more than enough for an average man but two was beyond the bounds of duty. He returned to our hotel late at night looking in remarkably good shape, considering his ordeal, and called for yoghurt and milk. Dairy products, as much as you can get, are the answer to drink, he proclaimed as he spooned down his yoghurt. They absorb the alcohol. Next morning he was absolutely fine.

On our last night, the GB–USSR held a banquet at the hotel attended by an uninvited guest. Robert Maxwell had flown in from Moscow at the last moment, had a place set for himself at the table, and had gone on to make a speech on Anglo-Soviet friendship. I wrote a piece about the uninvited guest in Siberia for the *Telegraph* diary. An angry Maxwell rang up Lord Hartwell and said he would sue the *Telegraph*, but that was the last we heard of the threat.

Moyra took to freelancing for the *Telegraph* and other publications, travelling across huge areas of the Soviet Union, writing human interest features that usually proved more readable than political coverage. On several occasions she assisted as a tour guide for a group of foreign wives living in Moscow. On one trip, down to the government vineyards in Azerbaijan, the group of about 25 was entertained to an outdoor lunch with lots of local wine. While Moyra stood up to reply to the toast of the estate's Armenian manager, the Bangladesh military attaché's wife sitting next to her, bent down to retrieve her napkin and alerted Moyra to a bug concealed under the table – doubtless intended to record any indiscretions of diplomatic wives.

The foreign women's trips were always a focus of attention for the local lads and one could never be sure which of them had been put up to it by the KGB. At a dinner at Yerevan, the 19-year-old daughter of an American businessman attracted the interest of a group of young Armenians who leapt aboard the group's midnight sleeper train to Tbilisi and gave the ladies an uneasy night trying to get into their compartments. *

It was a bit, Moyra said, like trying to run a rather overheated girl's school. Finally she went down the corridor to ask the carriage's woman guard – usually a fearsome breed – to get rid of the boys. But the guard was locked inside her van with her boyfriend and refused to come out.

KGB's Liaison Man

Ever since the death of Stalin there had been Kremlinologists predicting a thaw, but during our three years in Moscow, Stalinism remained alive and well.

It was easy for an old Moscow hand, returning after many years, to mistake signs of outward prosperity, and even the amazing appearance of private motor cars, with a loosening up of the system. Compared to the Khrushchev era, people were better dressed and better housed and society was more permissive. But hope was gone.

In the late 1950s and early 1960s there was oppression and intolerance but also a sense of excitement and change. Khrushchev would appear unexpectedly, sparking off at diplomatic receptions, even questioning sacred old party concepts. Thousands of Russians would flock to poetry readings of Yevgeny Yevtushenko and other protest poets whose subtle allusions to the purges and cruelties of the past were readily understood by their audience.

Under the neo-Stalinist regime of Brezhnev, the poetry readings were no more and Yevtushenko had become the court poet. His young audience, now middle-aged, had lost heart.

Russia's large Jewish community had also abandoned hope and, with a quiet US–Soviet détente deal worked out in the early 1970s by Henry Kissinger, were being allowed to depart at a rate of some 3,000 a month. Added to the normal Russian climate of anti-Semitism was now a reluctance to expend resources on training or promoting Russian Jews who were likely to take off for America or Israel at the first opportunity.

We attended a poignant farewell party for two of them, a husband and wife team and Moscow's wittiest satirical performers. Yevgeny Kozhevnikov and Olga Serova had become 'Refuseniks' and had been dismissed from their jobs when they applied to emigrate. Sir

Laurence Olivier and Sir John Gielgud had been among those who had appealed to Brezhnev to let them go. In the meantime, they had been putting on an underground satirical show in their small Moscow apartment to help keep up the morale of their 'Refusenik' friends.

They staged a final performance before leaving. Their only props were suitcases for departing emigrants, and the scene was Moscow's Sheremetyevo airport which they compared to 'a crematorium where people say goodbye forever'.

'Our forefathers used to leave Russia on foot, our fathers by train. We leave by planes from Sheremetyevo,' they sang. 'Jews have always been going away . . . Those who stayed behind went away in their dreams, and those that did leave used to return in their dreams.'

Departure is made in 'insulting haste' with no one to look after those left behind. 'Nowhere to go for a weep or a last kiss. But the day will come,' they sang, 'when it will be possible just to go to an airline counter and buy a ticket and go away and then come back when you feel like it.' Then an airport guide will say: 'Those are the stairs where the departing Jews used to ascend, and the balcony where they were not allowed to stand for more than five seconds to wave goodbye – forever. This is an historical monument preserved by the state. Please don't touch it with your hands.'

And in the most prominent position in the airport will be a statue 'to commemorate the old days of a Jew taking off, with only the tips of his toes touching the ground, his wife and children with suitcases holding on to his jacket, and two policemen hanging on to his legs.'

Some Russian Jews did, of course, survive and prosper. One of the best known to the Western press was Victor Louis – a millionaire by Soviet standards whose only official status appeared to be stringer for the *London Evening News* and a few other European papers. This was clearly insufficient to provide him with his Moscow apartment, his large *dacha* in the exclusive writer's colony in Peredelkino, his collection of eight antique cars including a vintage Bentley and a Mercedes, and a son at Oxford.

He was, in fact, the KGB's liaison man with the Western press, a leading purveyor of disinformation, with complete freedom to travel abroad. He was also the man who broke some of the most sensational news stories that came out of the Soviet Union. Despite his notoriety, he was mild-mannered, and quietly spoken and would have looked more at home running an antique shop on the King's Road (which his *dacha* somewhat resembled) than fulfilling the role of the Kremlin's *éminence grise*.

He was first with the story that Stalin's body was to be removed from Lenin's mausoleum, broke the news of the fall of Khrushchev, and was involved in shady efforts to discredit Stalin's daughter Svetlana, the author Alexander Solzhenitsyn and the dissident leader Andrei Sakharov.

His career was preceded by a spell in a Stalin *gulag* and, after his release, he successfully wooed Jennifer Statham, a young English graduate, when she was an au pair with the family of the British naval attaché in Moscow. This set the alarm bells ringing at the embassy and everything was done to try to dissuade Jennifer from marrying the man from the KGB. The assistant naval attaché warned her that if she married Victor, one day the KGB would call in the chips and use her. Years later, he told me, she sent him a card saying 'it never happened'.

The presence of Jennifer in the *dacha* certainly helped create the right social atmosphere for Victor to extend his contacts with the Western press and diplomats. We, among many others, would often drop in for a drink or Sunday lunch after a service at the Patriarch's lovely little church at Peredelkino. Diplomats and their wives either took Jennifer at face value, or viewed her as a traitor and snubbed her when she attended church services at the embassy.

Rather typically, Victor's last public appearance shortly before he died, was to attend Robert Maxwell's funeral in Jerusalem. Subsequently we visited Jennifer at her once safe and secure *dacha* to find that a fire had destroyed all Victor's cars, her next-door neighbour had been murdered by gangsters and she was living guarded by dogs behind newly installed high-security gates.

11

Afghanistan

Invasion

In the period of stagnation in the late 1970s, the steady decline in the Soviet economy coincided with a growing belligerence on the part of the Soviet Union's angry old leadership. There were all the signs of a break-up of the Soviet Union, but no Soviet experts, diplomats or journalists that I ever met predicted the speed or manner in which this vast communist empire would disintegrate – like that of its predecessor, Imperial Russia.

The popular view was that disintegration would begin, not in Moscow, but around the edges of the empire – the Caucasus, the Baltic and the Moslem republics – disenchanted with the collapse of the communist economy and the dead hand of the Kremlin. But with the overwhelming presence of the machinery of state terror and a standing army of over three million, it looked as though the Soviet Union would probably survive into the next millennium.

Its early demise was probably due more to Leonid Brezhnev and his hard-line advisers than to the reformist Mikhail Gorbachev. It was Brezhnev who upped the Cold War stakes in the late 1970s, gratuitously deploying his latest medium-range nuclear missiles against Western Europe and stirring up trouble throughout the Third World. And it was Brezhnev's fatal decision to re-enter the Great Game by invading Afghanistan on Christmas Eve, 1979, that was the defining moment.

President Carter and the West reacted strongly to the Kremlin's policy, first deploying *Cruise* and *Pershing* missiles in Western Europe and then boycotting the 1980 Moscow Olympics in response to the invasion of Afghanistan. But it was Jimmy Carter's successor Ronald Reagan, who denouncing Moscow as the 'Evil Empire', outspent the

Soviets in a new arms race, poured weapons into Afghanistan and helped bring the Soviet economy to its knees.

On arrival in Afghanistan, it was impossible not to see a parallel with America's disastrous involvement in Vietnam two decades earlier. The Americans, however, largely overcame the psychological effects of their defeat, while Soviet morale and confidence, already at a low ebb, never really recovered.

Unlike Vietnam, the Soviet people never saw the harrowing television coverage which chronicled the defeat of their forces at the hands of the Afghan guerrillas backed by the latest American military technology. They were only given the good news, but reality came to them in the return of their dead, or their living, demoralised and drug-addicted soldiers.

Within days of the Soviet invasion, the Moscow press corps was surprisingly being offered Afghan visas to visit Kabul. The Kremlin's motive behind this was to stage an international press conference held by its new puppet president in Afghanistan Babrak Karmal. Its aim was to give the world the impression of normality and legality in Afghanistan in advance of the UN debate on the Soviet invasion.

It was a chilling experience to arrive in Kabul and see Soviet tanks in the streets and Soviet troops freezingly encamped in tents around the capital of this, until recently, sovereign nation. One did not need much imagination to transfer the scene to one's own country under foreign occupation.

In arranging its public relations exercise, the Kremlin had a problem with its account of recent events. The official version was that Soviet forces had been sent in at the request of the government of President Hafizullah Amin which was threatened by reactionary Islamic Afghan elements backed by the imperialist powers, China and Pakistan.

What was more difficult to explain was why the Soviet special forces, flown in on Christmas Eve, promptly surrounded the presidential palace, attacked the guard, killed the president and replaced him with Karmal. As soon as the world press was assembled we were put on buses and driven to the presidential palace where soldiers were still clearing up the remains of the battle between Soviet forces and the presidential guard.

A distinctly uneasy Babrak Karmal, who had been living in exile in the Soviet Union and was brought in with the Soviet forces, did his best to assure us that everything was normal and legal, and that the Russian presence was entirely in accordance with the Soviet–Afghan

Treaty of Friendship. With tough censorship and no satellite communications available in those days, we managed to pigeon out some
accounts of the Soviet occupation with passengers flying to Delhi
and were then forced to leave as our 72-hour visas expired.

The invasion of Afghanistan was probably the last major international story before satellite communications became reasonably
available to the foreign press – thereby removing the heavy burden of
censorship which had always been one of the biggest obstacles to
foreign coverage.

On returning to Moscow, it occurred to me that the Afghan
embassy might not yet have had orders to stop issuing visas to correspondents now that we had fulfilled our function. Sure enough, they
gave me a new visa on the spot and the next night I was back at
Kabul airport facing an embarrassed Afghan army colonel in charge
of immigration who told me that absolutely no Western correspondents were being allowed in.

Bus Ride to Jalalabad

As there were no more flights that night, the colonel agreed that I
should be sent under guard to the Holiday Inn hotel in Kabul and
would be put on the first flight to New Delhi. The hotel, which two
days before had been packed with reporters and television teams, was
now eerily deserted. Several armed civilian communist youth students were in the lobby and one was assigned to me. He told me that
I was forbidden to leave the hotel and would be escorted to the airport the next morning.

Anxious to see what sort of control Soviet forces had outside
Kabul, I rose before dawn while my handler was still asleep. Leaving
the hotel, I made a dash for the bus station where I was joined by two
correspondents from AP and Reuters who had managed to stay on in
Kabul.

We decided to try to travel to Jalalabad along the road to the
Khyber Pass. The best way to get there and back in one piece, according to local advice at the bus station, was to take the 'Silver Bullet', a
battered silver Pakistan bus carrying an all-important green stripe of
the Prophet's colour. The local *mujahedin* freedom fighters liked
Pakistan and would be reluctant to fire on the bus, I was told. The
rival choice was a modern, secular, Afghan Tours Mercedes with huge
windows, offering both passengers, and snipers, a perfect view.
Sacrificing comfort for security, we cravenly chose the bus with the
mean windows.

Along with a five-piece Pakistani guitar band we sped down the Kabul gorge like the silver bullet of the bus's name, negotiating boulders rolled down the mountainside by the rebels, gaping holes in the mined road, felled trees and still smouldering trucks. Clearly, Soviet authority had its problems outside Kabul. Instructions in Pharsee cautioned 'In the presence of ladies do not use abusive language'. But the ladies were too smart to accompany us on this run.

At the entrance to Jalalabad we passed a Soviet T-54 tank lying in the river bed upturned by rebel forces, and rebels had blown up power pylons, cutting the city's electricity. Soviet attack helicopters flew low over the city and after the 8pm curfew I could hear tanks and armoured cars rumbling out to do battle with rebels who were attacking the nearby Soviet air base. Just after dawn, we saw an Afghan army truck filled with corpses heading back into town.

Later that day, rashly choosing the modern comforts of the Afghan Tours bus, we set out back to Kabul. Some 20 miles up the mountain – at about the point where in 1842 the last survivors of the once 16,000-strong retreating British expedition from Kabul met their end – we came under sniper fire and no longer relished our picture windows. We were soon joined by about 30 other trucks and buses which had been turned back on the way to Kabul.

The rebels, we were told, had set up a roadblock and were taking away and killing anyone suspected of being Russian or of supporting the ruling government party. I furtively hid my Aeroflot air ticket, made out in Cyrillic letters, under the carpet of the bus, but we were saved from being boarded by the arrival of two Afghan armoured cars which fired on the roadblock and escorted our convoy back to Jalalabad.

The next morning we returned to the bus station, but the bus driver seemed unenthusiastic about repeating the experiences of the previous day. He said he was waiting for a tank to escort us and it might be some days before it turned up. The only alternative was an old wreck of a Volga taxi with a driver who looked villainous beyond belief. With faint hearts we set out for Kabul – an eerie experience. Unlike the previous days the road was totally deserted.

At about the point where we had been fired on, our driver pulled up outside a dilapidated Afghan *chaikhana* (tea house), pretending to repair a long broken temperature gauge. Suddenly we were surrounded by a group of glowering *mujahedin*. It was clear that our driver had delivered us to them – and that if they decided we were Russians they would make short work of us.

One was fingering a long, very thin blade of steel which disappeared into the folds of his sleeve. 'British,' we said hopefully. But they continued to glower. 'English, Anglistan.' Still no result, but they seemed to be closing in. In desperation, I cried 'You know, British, BBC.'

That was the magic word that did it. 'Ah BBC. Very good. Thank you,' they shouted. We all shook hands, and we were soon on our way back to Kabul.

An Old Crow

I returned to Moscow on the day of the arrest of Andrei Sakharov, whose denunciation of the invasion of Afghanistan was the last straw for Brezhnev. Hearing rumours of his disappearance, a group of us went round to his apartment, to find it locked with plainclothes KGB men barring our entrance. He and his wife had been whisked off to Gorky, one of the cities forbidden to foreigners, and Sakharov was held there for several years until Mikhail Gorbachev brought him back in the heady days of *perestroika*.

The exile of Sakharov added to a general feeling of gloom and depression. More than 60 years of communism since the Bolshevik Revolution had managed to produce an increasingly petrified and isolated society, where any individual genius or talent was stifled or driven abroad. With nothing to show except an increasingly menacing military machine, the Soviet leadership was now turning to the Moscow Olympics to try to improve the image of a nation that now no one else wanted to emulate.

Churches and cathedrals were being gilded, buildings on the route from the airport were being painted for the first time in years. Intourist was preparing to do its usual job of beguiling the foreign visitor, while the Russians, as always, were being warned to beware of being contaminated by capitalist travellers from the West.

The Olympics themselves, boycotted by the West, became a façade for a sad society. The spirit of the occasion had been destroyed by the territorial greed of the old Kremlin leaders who were themselves drifting towards extinction.

In the midst of these depressing, late winter days in Moscow, the *Telegraph* called me. Steve Barber had died unexpectedly at the age of 58 and they wanted me to return to Washington to take over the bureau and prepare to cover the 1980 US elections.

On the Sunday before our departure we set out for Peredelkino for a last visit to the church and to say goodbye to Victor Louis and his wife. But on the way we saw Jennifer Louis driving into Moscow. The English wife of the man from the KGB was at the wheel of

Victor's 1930 Bentley. She was on her way to a church service held in the study of the British ambassador's residence, overlooking the Kremlin, and conducted by Eric Staples, a chaplain to the Queen.

There was another Russian vignette that has stuck in my mind from our last days in Moscow. The spring thaw had just started and, walking beside the Moskva river, I watched an evil-tempered Russian crow squawking at two ducks sharing the same ice floe. These flocks of crows are often portrayed in old Russian pictures, ominously circling above a church or graveyard, and this one, having driven off the ducks, stood on the edge of the ice, with neck outstretched, still cursing them.

Not satisfied with occupying a sheet of ice as big as a tennis court, the crow wanted to control the water around it. Defiance, ill-temper and territorial greed had been a feature of the Soviet Union and its ageing leadership during my three years in Moscow. And I was left with a very Russian image of that raucous and angry old bird, drifting down the river in the thaw.

Bibliography

Adams Schmidt, Dana, *Yemen. The Unknown War*. Holt, Rinehart & Winston, New York (1968)

Aitken, Jonathan, *Nixon: A Life*. Weidenfeld & Nicolson, London (1993)

An Autobiography of King Hussein of Jordan, *Uneasy Lies the Head*. Heinemann, London (1962)

Binyon, Michael, *Life in Russia*. Hamish Hamilton, London (1983)

Bushell, Terry, *Marriage of Inconvenience*. André Deutsch, London (1985)

Coleman, Fred, *The Decline and Fall of the Soviet Empire*. St Martin's Press, New York (1996)

Cruise O'Brien, Connor, *To Katanga and Back*. Hutchinson, London (1962)

Emery, Fred, *Watergate. The Corruption and Fall of Richard Nixon*. London (1994)

Hart-Davies, Duff, *The House the Berrys Built*. Hodder & Stoughton, London (1990)

Karnow, Stanley, *Vietnam: A History* . Pimlico, London (1994)

Mansfield, Peter, *A History of the Middle East*. Penguin Books, London (1992)

Pasha, Glubb, *A Soldier with the Arabs*. Hodder & Stoughton, London (1959)

Philby, Kim, *My Secret War*. MacGibbon & Key, London (1968)

Wharton, Michael, *A Dubious Codicil. An Autobiography*. Chatto & Windus, London (1991)

Index

171